Arguing at the Crossroads

Edited by

Paul Brennan & Catherine de Saint Phalle

ARGUING at the CROSSROADS

ESSAYS ON A CHANGING IRELAND

NEW ISLAND BOOKS

Arguing at the Crossroads
was first published in Ireland in June 1997
by
New Island Books,
2 Brookside,
Dundrum Road,
Dublin 14,
Ireland.

Copyright ©

ISBN 1 874597 545

It was originally published as **Désirs D'Irlande**, ©
Actes Sud-AFAA, Paris, 1996 (Association française
d'action artistique, ministère des affaires étrangères)

New Island Books receives financial assistance from
The Arts Council (An Chomhairle Ealaíon),
Dublin, Ireland.

Cover design by Jon Berkeley
Typeset by YellowStone
Printed in Ireland by Colour Books, Ltd.

ACKNOWLEDGEMENTS

Julia O'Faolain's essay, *The Imagination As Battlefield*, is copyright Julia O'Faolain. Reproduced by permission of the author c/o Rogers, Coleridge & White Ltd., 20 Powis Mews, London W11 1 JN.

Angela Bourke's essay, *Language, Stories, Healing*, is to appear in Anthony Bradley and Maryann Valiulis, eds., *Gender and Sexuality in Modern Ireland* (Boston: University of Massachusetts Press). It is printed here by permission of the Press and of the American Conference for Irish Studies. The author also gratefully acknowledges the permission of Professor Bo Almqvist, Department of Irish Folklore, University College, Dublin, and of Peadar Ó Ceannabháin, editor, *Éamon a Búrc: Scéalta* to publish the story translation.

The other essays are reproduced with the permission of Actes Sud, and of the authors.

CONTENTS

1. **Introduction:**
   Doireann Ní Bhriain — 9

2. **Imagining Ireland:**
   Eavan Boland — 13

3. **The Imagination as Battlefield:**
   Julia O'Faolain — 24

4. **Imagining Conamara:**
   Bob Quinn — 44

5. **Language, Stories, Healing:**
   Angela Bourke — 58

6. **Perpetual Motion:**
   Fintan O'Toole — 77

7. **Everything is Political in a Divided Society:**
   John Hume — 98

8. **Irish Art, An Art of Journeying and Dislocations:**
   Liam Kelly — 107

9. **Thou Shalt Not Kill:**
   John Banville — 132

10. **Irish Music:**
    Fintan Vallely — 143

Introduction

This collection of essays was first published in France under the title *Desirs d'Irlande*. It was one of several books published as part of L'Imaginaire Irlandais, a festival of contemporary Irish culture held in France in the first half of 1996.

The word festival was something of a misnomer. We used it as shorthand to describe a series of events, publications and connections which were to put some of the vibrancy of contemporary Irish cultural activity before a French public in a concentrated way over a six-month period.

The idea had come from President Mary Robinson who in a conversation with the late French President François Mitterand in 1992 had remarked on how little of our contemporary cultural activity had been seen in France. She knew how the French loved Ireland, but felt they were unaware of how much was happening on the cultural scene in recent years. Four years later, we went some way towards filling that gap in French perceptions.

Shortly after the French commissioner, Michel Ricard, and I began work on the project in late 1993, we agreed that it would best serve Ireland's interest if we were to persuade French institutions to include work from Ireland in their cultural programming in 1996. Our task, therefore, was to introduce them to what was happening in Ireland and to work with them in bringing some of what they saw and heard to new French audiences.

We felt very strongly that events alone would not fully justify the effort and financial expenditure involved. France, and particularly Paris, regularly plays host to other cultures and we were anxious not to be just another.

As with all the elements of l'Imaginaire Irlandais, decisions about content were made jointly with our French partners in the cultural institutions and publishing houses. For a while, this seemed something of a handicap to us on the Irish side. Then as relationships developed between the French and Irish cultural worlds it began to make complete sense. The French institutions after all were the ones taking the programming and publishing risks — although we were giving them a certain amount of financial help — and they knew better than we did what might interest their audiences. It was a curious and indeed instructive experience for the Irish side to see Ireland and its cultural output through French eyes. We did not always agree with their views and there were many lively debates and the inevitable compromises. We were very pleased with the outcome, however, and felt very proud of what turned out to be the final programme of l'Imaginaire Irlandais.

Actes Sud, who were a real pleasure to deal with, were very open to our ideas on how to prepare this book. They wisely decided to appoint joint editors, one French and one Irish. The French editor, novelist Catherine de St Phalle, had already fallen in love with Ireland and indeed had set one of her novels here. The Irish editor, Paul Brennan, Professor of Irish Studies in Caen University, has lived and taught in France for many years. He has done remarkable work in developing the field of Irish studies in French universities and was ideally suited to the task.

The cover of the French edition of this collection sports a photograph of a freckled Irish child with red curly hair and a winning smile. This, it was explained to us, was the image most likely to attract a French hibernophile audience. My initial displeasure eventually turned to satisfaction as I realised how effectively the texts would subvert that simple image.

Each of the nine writers who contributed to this book added another dimension to l'Imaginaire Irlandais. The

Introduction

range of voices and ideas addressed in this collection conveyed something of the richness and diversity of contemporary Ireland to our French audience. I hope that they will also be seen as a valuable contribution to the ongoing debates and exchanges taking place in this island about who we are and where we should be going.

Doireann Ní Bhriain
Irish Commissioner for L'Imaginaire Irlandais
May 1997

Imagining Ireland

Eavan Boland

I was born in Ireland in the city of Dublin. My father was a Dubliner, my mother was not. We lived on a leafy road near the centre of the city, in a house with a lilac tree almost blocking the gate. Nearby was a canal with its green, raggy banks and its splintered wooden locks. Within a five minute walk was Grafton Street and St. Stephen's Green.

By the time I was born, the Irish state was more than twenty years old and within five years of becoming the Republic its patriots had dreamed of and died for. It was enclosed in the struggle to remain neutral in the Second World War. But if I try to imagine the city as it was then I come up with little more than a grey and intimate place, with a witty and malicious literary life, set in a cup of hills with the coast all around it. A place with little traffic, endless rain, a culture of gossip and verbal exuberance.

These days I drive by those areas once a week. The house I lived in is set back from the road and has been divided into offices but the lilac tree is still there. The canal is unchanged. The city is still within walking distance, but it is a different city.

I lived in that house until I was five years of age. Then I moved with my family to London and lived there until I was twelve. The changes involved in the move from country to country were enormous, far more than the few hundred miles between two cities would suggest. To start with, there were differences of food and weather and clothing and schooling. Those were the immediate changes. The puddings tasted odd and the fog was thick and strange. The buses were red and not green. The post boxes were red as well.

There was also — but I was a child and could only have noticed this at the most basic and animal level — a change in the light. The coastal brightness of Dublin had given way to the post-war gloom of London. There were other dislocations; less obvious perhaps, but just as painful. After a while, my speech changed, My mouth filled up with word-sounds which looked the same on the page, but were different in their rising and falling intonations, which I learned to imitate but which were never really my own.

Those were the obvious changes. When I look back now I realise there was another one, which I never registered at the time but which would come to influence a great deal of the way I thought about my childhood. Quite simply, the word *Ireland* changed. A single word. Until I moved away, went to London, began to absorb different weather and strange food, the word *Ireland* had been almost invisible. No one spoke the word because no one needed to. It was everywhere. It was the noun that implied both adjective and ownership. For those five years, before I left my country, it was a hard-working and yet ordinary word, accomplishing every day the task it had been made for. The name of my country. Just that. Nothing more.

Then I went away, lost my access to a place and suddenly the word was everywhere. It was in front of me, being spelled out in black crayons on the tied parcels my mother was sending to the post. It was on an envelope from America, arriving in the morning post. And suddenly, also, quite without warning it became a dangerous word, a word signifying what no child wants — a difference from others. I learned that one day when I was about seven. I was waiting to put my coat on downstairs in the school cloakroom. I was getting ready to be collected. A teacher came in, her face set and impatient. She told me to hurry up, 'I amn't going yet,' I said to her, using the Irish not the English form of the negative contraction. Her reaction was angry, immediate, unforgettable. She whirled around. 'You're not in Ireland now,' she said. It was my first glimpse of the power and locale of language, and the pain of estrangement.

Because I was distant from my country, I spent much of my childhood imagining it. This would never have happened if I had stayed in Ireland. Then I would have taken it for granted, lived into it, and, in an important sense, stayed out of it. As it was I tried to read myself back into it. I attached to it fragments of history and rumour. I found out about its fractured narrative of heroes, the ballads, the sacrifices, the songs; and I never questioned it. What I could not discover, I invented. Ironically, freedom to do so was greater than if I had remained in my own country, bound by the actuality and truth of its place, its people, its food, its place-names.

I came back to Ireland when I was fourteen. I saw unfamiliar sights; horses and lamplight and the muddy curve of the Liffey. I grew to know street names and bus timetables. I went to live with my sisters in a flat outside the city. I went to boarding school. I studied for exams. I started again to explore the word *Irish*: not this time as a distant fact, but as the close-up reality of my surroundings. As a word which painted letter-boxes and coloured trains. Which framed laws and structured language.

Ireland, Irish, Ours. If I could not remember a country, I could at least imagine a nation. I was not searching for a dialogue. I was looking to disappear into powerful images: the narrow backways of a British town where a shot was fired, a man was captured and the refrain of a ballad was made inevitable. Of a channel of water where French sailing ships creaked and heaved. Of a gibbet, its outline visible for miles against a Wexford horizon.

There was an intense attraction about the way these pictures of action and faith re-constructed their reader into a more fervent and simple intelligence. Within that re-construction — although this was only an instinctive sense — the years of dislocation could be healed by entering the story.

And it was not just a story of place. It was also a story of heroes. The heroes were cast — in ballad after ballad, chapter after chapter — in a recognisable mould. Either they were singular and dangerous, armed with a gun and a bomb, facing the enormity of a task: the blowing up of a granite bridge, the assassination of a Field-Marshal. Or else they were eloquent and doomed: facing a corrupt court, keeping a journal as the prison ship steamed out of Dublin Bay, past a beloved line of hills and the lights of an Irish summer morning. I wanted to belong to all that.

But I could not. I came back to Ireland at fourteen years of age to find that my vocabulary of belonging was missing. The street names, the meeting places — it was not just that I did not know them. It was something more; I had never known them. I had lost not only a place, but the past that goes with it, and, with it, the clues from which to construct a present self.

I had to learn a new sensory idiom. The taste of a fog which was different from the London one: less gritty, with more of an ocean aftertaste. An unkempt greenness on the streets. A drizzle which was inter-seasonal, constant. Different trees. Different birds.

As I learned these things, the last unwanted gift of exile came to me. I began to watch places with an interest so exact it might have been memory. There was that street-corner, with the small newsagent which sold copies of the *Irish Independent* and square honeycombs in summer. I could imagine myself there, a child of nine, buying Peggy's leg and walking back down by the Canal, the lock brown and splintered as ever, the young boys diving from it.

It became a powerful impulse. This slow and intense reconstruction of a childhood which had never happened. A fragrance or a trick of light was enough. Or a house I entered which I wanted not just to appreciate but remember; and then I would begin. Here was the hall with its parquet floor, the sideboard with white lilac and gilded mirror. There were the photographs of the children and the kennel outside for the dog. I had been eleven here, playing with a friend in that garden. I had been six. I could remember the croquet game in summer, the skirts of women, the serious and intent faces of the players.

There was a small seaside town outside Drogheda called Clogher Head. I had missed it by a small action, by a form of words. Now I thought myself back into it. Summer days when the rain cleared and the roads were vacant. A bicycle lying sideways on the main street, and a brown and white dog barking. Red lemonade sold in long bottles. And the vista full of bathers and fishing boats, and the grit of sand as it came out of shoes and towels. And I, in a room where light came through the curtain until an hour before midnight, lying down to sleep. An Irish child.

There is something poignant about all this in retrospect. It has something to do with language and imagination, and how one can actually distort the other. The word *Ireland* should have been the name of my childhood. Instead it became the name of my hope, my invention, my longing. I learned to consider the word, to repeat it to myself, in circumstances of estrangement. I read into it acts of heroism and history. I took out of it a clear and definite chronicle into which I came to believe if I was careful and strong-minded, I could re-enter my own name. I was aware even then at the end of my childhood that this word had angles and edges which were different from other words. That these vowels were more glamorous and demanding. What I did not want, as I finished that long and unhappy exile of my childhood, was to find myself again at odds with that word Ireland. Again estranged from it. Again at a loss as to how to enter a claim to its power and distinction.

But that is exactly what happened. Or what I thought happened. I went to college, began to write poetry and began to publish it. As a student and a young poet I drank coffee and talked about literature in the centre of the city, inside the shelter of pubs and libraries and college rooms where poetry seemed an unquestioned and honoured undertaking. I had a flat full of books and coffee cups which was hardly a mile away from the canal and the lilac tree where I had first grown up. The painful distances of my childhood were long forgotten. I felt connected again. I felt part — I was too young to question the concept — of a literary tradition. I felt the excitement — again this was part of being young — of having the chance to add to it. The word Irish in front of the word poetry or literature felt like an answer now, rather than a question or an enigma. I did not want and I did not seek out any more questions.

But they came anyway. I married in my early twenties. I left the flat I lived in. I packed up my books and went, in the dead of winter, to a suburb only four miles away from the centre but light years away from its concerns. The road was raw and partially unbuilt. The street lamps were not yet connected. No one had the time to sit and drink coffee and talk about poetry or tradition. I was about to learn, all over again, how place and distance can affect language.

That first spring, however, I thought of little else but practicalities. Ovens and telephones became images and emblems of the real world. The house was cold. We had no curtains. At night, the lights on the hills furnished the upper rooms with a motif of adventure and estrangement. In the morning, the hills marched in, close or distant, promising rain or the dry breezes of a March day.

If I had looked about me with a wider sense of curiosity I would have noticed more. To start with, I would have seen a past as well as a present. I was oblivious, for instance, to the fact that Dundrum, this village four miles from the centre, had its roots in Anglo-Norman times, when the castle had first been built to ward off the Wicklow clans. Its destiny as a residential centre had been settled centuries later, when the Harcourt street railway line was opened. With its assistance, the distance between

Dundrum and the city centre became a mere sixteen minutes.

It was all changing by the time we arrived. Indeed the arrival of young couples like ourselves was a signal of that change. But enough distinction remained to give a sense of the grace and equilibrium of the place it had been. Granted, the farriers at the corner of the village had been gone some twenty years. But the cobbler remained. Further down, the experiment of a mink farm had failed and a shopping centre was in the process of replacing it. Above all, the location remained, the wonderful poise of the village at the edge of theatrical, wooded cliffs and under the incline of the Dublin mountains.

Occasionally I would be aware of the contradictions and poignance of our new home. But in the main I missed the fact that the shops, the increasing traffic, the lights on the hills and we ourselves were not isolated pieces of information. They and we were part of a pattern: one that was being repeated throughout Ireland in those years. Before our eyes, and because of them, a village was turning into a suburb.

Summers came and went and trees began to define the road. Garden walls were put up and soon enough the voices calling over them on long, bright evenings, the bicycle thrown on its side, and the single roller skate, belonged to my children. Somewhat to my surprise, I had done what most human beings have done, I had found a world and I had populated it.

And yet it did not exist on any known map. This place with its cars, its exhaust fumes, its clipped hedges and exuberant children could not be found in any breviary of Irish poetry or any catalogue of Irish history. It was not the place my childhood, with its romance and invention, had prepared me for. It was not the place my adolescent years had prepared me to find. It was a downright and actual world. Its emergencies were not national or literary. They did not seem to belong, and they had not been predicted, by that engagement with the word Ireland which had so preoccupied me when I was younger. This place seemed on the one hand, too local, and, on the other, too universal to go with what I had come to think of as a national literature and a national identity.

But in this suburban house, nevertheless, at the foothills of the Dublin mountains, married and with two little daughters, I led a life which would have been recognizable to any woman who had led it and to many others who had not. My days were arrayed with custom and necessity, acts so small their momentousness was visible to no one but myself. Season by season, I separated cotton from wool and the bright digits of gloves from ankle-socks. I drove the car. I collected children from school. In spring, the petals from across the road blew down, strewing the kerbs with the impression of a summer wedding. In February, after a high wind, the village street was littered with slates.

But at night the outer landscape yielded to an inner one. Familiar items blanked out and were replaced by others. The street lamp stood in for the whitebeam tree, the planet of rain around it displaced the rowan berries. And in those darknesses, I lay down as conscious of the love for my children as I would have been of a sudden and chartless fever. And conscious also of how that love spread out from the bed on which I lay, and out further to the poplar trees, to the orange plastic mug at one side of the hedge, to the glint of a bicycle wheel and the half-moon.

I understood then, as any human being would, the difference between love and a love which is visionary. The first may well be guaranteed by security and attachment, only the second has the power to transform. As I lay there, my mind went seeking well beyond the down-to-earth and practical meaning of a daily love. The apple trees. the rustle and click of shadow-leaves. The mysterious cycle of plants. In those darknesses it could seem to me that this was not a world in which my love happened, but one whose phenomenology occurred because of it.

Poetry is full of such transformations. They are, for example, the weather of most love poems. They constitute much of the perspective of the great conventions, such as the pastoral. I ought to have felt that my experiences, even my half-formed impressions at this time, connected well with my training as a poet. But I did not. As each morning came around, with its fresh sights and senses, I felt increasingly the distance between my own life, my lived experience, and conventional interpretations both of poetry and the poet's life. It was not exactly or even chiefly that the recurrences of my world — a child's face, the dial of a washing machine — were absent from the tradition, although they were. It was not even so much that I was a woman. It was that, being a woman, I had entered into a life for which poetry has no name.

But the namelessness did not stop at the poetry. As I looked out my window at the suburb what did I see? I saw whitebeam trees and roofs. I saw the blue mountains of the Dublin hills and behind them the outline of the Wicklow hills. I saw the new lives that Irish people were living against the infinitely old weather and landscape of the country which had entered their lives, which was marked on their passports, but which might well stop short of their imaginations. I began to brood on what it might mean to imagine a country; and what it might mean to fail to imagine it.

It is much easier to make your identity and, if you are a poet, your poetry, from the past and not the present. When I was a student, when I was a child, I took some comfort and some strength from repeating the word Ireland to myself. It was a word which had been made by maps, by memories, by emigrant songs and acts of heroism. It was a well-defined place which invited a feeling of belonging. But when I tried to belong to that place I was filled with an unformed doubt: a doubt which gradually became an unease at my own longing for certainty and inclusion. And now as I looked out the window, I felt like a map-maker who finds that an old and well-loved map is inaccurate in several respects.

I had after all, begun writing poetry in a city where the life of the poet, like the name of a nation, was confined to a few well understood habits of love and recovery. As dusk fell in the city, conversational life intensified. Libraries filled up; the great cowled lamps went on and light pooled onto open pages. The pubs were crowded. The cafés were full of students and apprentice writers like myself, some of them talking about literature, a very few talking intensely about poetry.

Only a few miles away was the almost invisible world that everyone knew of and no one referred to. Of suburbs and housing estates. Of children and women. Of fires lighted for the first winter chill, of food put on the table. No one referred to this. The so-called ordinary world, which most of us had come from and some would return to on the last bus, was not even mentioned. Young poets are like children. They assume the dangers to themselves are those their elders identified. They internalise the menace without analysing it. It was not said, it was not even consciously thought and yet I absorbed the sense that poetry was safe here in this city at twilight, with its violet sky and constant drizzle, within this circle of libraries and pubs and talked about stanzas and cadences. Beyond it was the ordinariness which could only dissipate it; beyond it was a life for which no visionary claim could be made.

This inconvenient and unglamorous place, where the rain fell coldly on new houses, was not marked on any map I knew, physical, imaginative or literary. It was not that I felt someone, or even myself, should mark it on such a map. It was that its exclusion must call the very act of cartography into question. Sometimes, on my way to call in a child in the evening — although I am reconstructing these thoughts with more precision than they ever could have occurred with — I looked about me thoughtfully at the small street, the corner that it disappeared into, the way houses crowded and repeated one another. This was not a figurative place. No gallows had been built there. No ballad named it. No historian was likely to come looking for its past. But it happened. It was continuing to happen even as I looked at it. I lived there, I knew that.

And yet there was a certain temptation to leave this awkward and unnamed place, where my life had happened, at the very edges of that word, Ireland. To honour the dreams and hungers of my childhood and regard this new actual landscape as one that I need not struggle to incorporate in those old dreams. And that, I reflected, must after all be the map-maker's greatest temptation. To leave the drawing of a place in the most interesting and evocative shape. Not to include the new and difficult realities in case they disturbed the old.

The more I thought it however, the more I began to be fascinated not so much by the way we make a word, as the way a word re-makes our world. *Ireland*. I had lived in the way others had made that word. I had seen it re-make my reality. Now I wanted to continue the process.

And here I leave this story. I did indeed include that world outside my window in the map I made. I included it in the poems I wrote. I added it to the new Ireland. We have no way of living in a place, we have no way of belonging to that place, unless we continue to imagine it.

The Imagination as Battlefield

Julia O'Faolain

Now that we have all drawn closer, how recognize 'Irishness'? Or indeed 'Frenchness'? Such notions often tell more about the perceiver than about the perceived.

'How French' we sometimes still say of arguments which seem too airily abstract. What *that* tells you is that we — by whom I mean the Anglophones, the English and those of us who speak their language — are more comfortable when things are rooted in the particular. The language cleaves to it and, moreover, we Irish have our own reasons for craving accuracy. We do so in reaction against generations of Celtic rhetoricians whose windiness is now out of fashion, because we have had a surfeit of slogans and, last but not least, because of the gossip or tale-bearer who lives inside many of us. I mean 'tale-bearer' in a good sense, for where would our fiction-writers have been without the source material which was provided by sharp-eyed, curtain-twitching, small-town observers? Almost all the great-grandparents of today's Irish bourgeoisie lived repressed lives in gossipy places, which is why we, like them, have a feel for a good anecdote or scandal and agree with Flaubert that God is in the detail.

It's the policeman in us too. It is well known that the jobs which first enabled the cleverer children of the ordinary Irish peasantry to better themselves were in school teaching and the police force plus, to be sure, the Roman Catholic Church. Priests, policemen and schoolteachers are niggling folk and you'll find them in most native Irish backgrounds. As a result, many of us were brought up to be good witnesses, respect precision, delight in realism and enjoy a laugh at bureaucratic diction. This shows up in our fiction as well as in our jokes.

'Can the witness say with assurance whether on the night in question the defendant was sufficiently sober to recognise that the victim of his assault was a law officer?' We love guying this sort of rural cop-talk. 'Was the officer's state of undress such as to constitute entrapment?'

Centuries of familiarity with the confessional give you a relish for such situations, an ear tuned to pedantry and an appreciation of ironies and degrees of bad faith. There is also some half-tender mockery here for those laborious and simple old cops of long ago.

The cop, a figure emblematic of our past divisions, turns up a lot in Irish writing, and indeed, even as I write this, a new Irish play on the theme is completing a successful run in London. *The Steward of Christendom* brilliantly exploits the pathos of a police officer who, having risen as high in the old Royal Irish Constabulary 'as a Catholic could' — the phrase is telling — finds himself reviled when, behind his back as it were, in 1921, nationalism changes the value system. Once Ireland achieves independence, he and his family, who were until then widely respected citizens, are regarded as collaborators with the Crown. Traitors. People who failed to turn their coats fast enough. The play, by Sebastian Barry, is based on the story of a relative of his own and I, whose grandfather was also in the RIC, find it richly resonant — the more so as my grandfather's three sons went, respectively, and incompatibly into the Catholic Church, the British Civil Service and the IRA. To which of their memories should I now deny sympathy?

Divisions, fractures and having an uncomfortable conscience on account of them are part of our heritage. And it is for this reason too that many of us, I contend, yearn for realism and cling to particulars.

On the other hand — I hope I am not soon going to find myself needing as many hands as the Goddess Kali — some of us revel some of the time in a punning pedantry which dissolves precision into multiplicity and joke. That, surely, comes from our clerical education. Take the title of a famous French play by a famous Irish writer, *En attendant Godot*. To an English speaker 'Godot' evokes God. An Irish critic has, as a variant pun, suggested the Gaelic *go deo* meaning 'forever', which reinforces Beckettian — and Irish — pessimism since the title then becomes 'Waiting forever'. Well, why not? But equally — I don't know whether anyone has previously suggested this — why not the Italian *'godo'* from the verb *godere* meaning *jouir*? The title then becomes 'I enjoy while I wait' or even, to use a more everyday English word, 'I come while I wait' which punningly, starts to turn the title into what is called 'an Irish bull' or a contradiction in terms, thus effacing meaning by providing too much of it.

The above is an example of our imagination at play, forcing the rabbit of reality back inside the conjuror's hat. Therapy? Perhaps. It is an old, idle game which I learned in my childhood from unemployed men sitting in bus shelters and outside pubs during closing time: proto-Vladimirs and Estragons. I suspect that long before then groups of similar men, afflicted with a surfeit of leisure, must have played word-games to kill time, mirroring the vacancy of their lives in ingenious chit-chat while their women got on with the housework. Probably they couldn't go home until they had spent some hours pretending to look for work — there never has been enough of that in Ireland — and, having no hope of controlling their lives, they were taking their revenge on words. As a literary sport it seems, even now, to appeal exclusively to men. At all events, I can think of no Irish woman writer who engages in it in a sustained way. The Irish psyche, as Irish social gatherings used to do until fairly recently, has a tendency to divide on lines of gender. Our female novelists are all, broadly speaking, realists. But then, the playful imposition of subversive or ingeniously controlling devices on narrative has been a male game in most countries.

Let me speculate as to why.

Eagerness to take control makes some people afraid to take airplanes. They distrust the pilot. Masterful people suffer most. Analogously, masterful male writers, foiled in their efforts to totally control either external reality or the phantasmagoria inside their heads, have in our pluralist and shifty times evolved various sorts of anti-novel and auto-destructive modes of narration whose tricksiness makes the narrative vehicle's plausibility explode. The realist convention is thus violated, parodied, shown up and taken apart for the reader's greater enjoyment. Reality's elusiveness — like the passenger's inability to take over the plane — is thereby acknowledged, but distress is soothed by the brilliance with which this is done. The reader will know which international writers fit this pattern. In Ireland the obvious names are Beckett, Joyce, Flann O'Brien, John Banville and, most recently, Michael Collins. I hasten to say that I find them all dazzlingly entertaining — and assuaging. The pent-up spirit needs a safety valve, an occasional puff of cleverly released steam.

Our women, though, are, as I said, more classical in their approach, less self-reflexive or insistently knowing, although the novels of Jennifer Johnston — to take just one — have a parable-like inventiveness and can sometimes seem to be simultaneously telling a story and commenting on it, both re-using and exploding old paradigms as when, in *The Invisible Worm*, she shows her heroine, a member of the Anglo-Irish gentry on her mother's side, burning down the summerhouse where her father abused her as a child. The father is native Irish, so the act both privatises and cuts down to size that grand old narrative ritual: the burning of Anglo-Irish big houses by native revolution- aries. More of these houses must by now have been burned in Irish novels than in Irish history, but Johnston's shrinking of the event to domestic proportions renews the rather tired plot by taking the romanticism out of it. Delicately, moreover, this miniaturising throws fresh light on an old theme: the friction between two sorts of Irish people, the gentry and the peasantry. Her novel, by making the violence incestuous, emphasises the closeness and pain of their old, baleful feud as well as the difficulty of ending it since the marriages she describes between members of the opposing tribes bring no happiness. Her ingenious, pessimistic plotting seems to me very Irish indeed.

Men v. women, gentry v. peasantry, unionists v. nationalists, Celtic revivalists versus those who would rather forget the old myths or turn them upside down, people who feel defensive about writing in English rather than Irish or who feel defensive about the sort of English in which they write — 'Hiberno' or British — versus those eager to be free of such concerns — these and other divisions make the typical state of the Irish imagination seem to be schism.

Even physically we are divided for, apart from Partition — the division of North from South — we have an enormous diaspora. There are far more of us abroad than there are in Ireland, and this affects us because there is a great deal of going back and forth and a lot of reciprocal influence so that, paradoxically, constant rejoining and re-gathering heightens our consciousness both of belonging and of separation. The wound has no time to heal nowadays for, as air travel has shrunk the world, the break is rarely final or clean. Yet families are still being scattered by emigration and, on visits to old people's homes in Ireland, I have been more than once waylaid by inmates complaining of loneliness and lamenting the loss of daughters who went abroad to marry or to work. Perhaps I reminded them of those lost women?

Our present is variously haunted.

The Imagination as Battlefield

Sitting in, say, the London Underground or at a party in the US Consulate in Florence, I often see faces I knew from my childhood: Irish features recognisable in a foreign crowd. It is an elusive perception because of what I gather is now called 'ethnic fade'. This is the phenomenon whereby emigrants lose their original identity and fade into the host population. They take on its ways, and their personalities change and so do their faces. And yet, the distinctive bones and skin colours persist so that reincarnations of ancestral ghosts will fleetingly reappear even in third-generation emigrants. They are hallucinatingly recognisable, yet hard to describe since the Celts are not so very different from other Europeans. Daniel O'Connell, the 19th-century 'Liberator', has peered at me from a drunk's face outside a London flophouse and, from under a delicatessen saleswoman's white, hygienic hat; a dead ringer for my grandmother asked impatiently whether I wanted my Italian sausages with red pepper or without.

It is the same with our mental world. One has moments of recognition. 'How Irish' people say of us if we produce an 'Irish bull' or talk too much about the past or see the future in terms of it or insist, to English embarrassment, on paying more than our share because we can't bear to see friends splitting minute sums and fussing over how much to tip. This shames us. We don't mind being or seeming poor, but blush to seem mean and are — until the ethnic fade sets in — hospitable and tribal.

Such stereotypes afflict and affect us. For how throw them off? If I look in the mirror and see that my face is beginning to look like my mother's I cannot but feel differently about her. She now dwells inside me as I once did in her. But parent-child relations were tricky for those of us whose parents had excitedly forged for themselves an identity whose newness made it dubious, like a mask with a tendency to slip. In my own case my parents' nationalism led them, in their ardent teen years, which were also the teen years of this century, to embrace a disappearing Gaelic heritage by going to study it in the Western mountains where people still spoke the language. Later my father joined the IRA and the national struggle and learned to make bombs. Theirs was a voluntary, indeed an ecstatic, assumption of a culture which had not been taught in their schools. However, by the time I reached school in 1940, Independence was twenty years old and that culture was official. Gaelic, being now obligatory, was no longer romantic, and learning it was pure drudgery. Civic freedoms were restricted and the Free State government was using the nationalist myths which had brought it to power in order to still all opposition and criticism. Identifying itself with Irishness, it — like the people in Sebastian Barry's play — branded opponents traitors and 'West Britons'. So where, for my generation, was conformism? Freedom? An identity of our own? The imaginative wells had been tampered with.

We could not go back, however, to being like our grandparents. We were glad to be living in an independent Irish state, whatever its imperfections, for we did not feel English. However affable the English people we met, they felt alien. Their history and especially their reading of our history were to blame and no doubt so was the Protestant temperament. Their sensibility, snobberies and values have to this day made some of their favourite great novels impossible for me to love in the way I love Russian and French ones. The high-principled smugness of George Eliot, for instance, makes my skin crawl.

Such reactions can seem trivial but I, if I am to be as particular as I can, have to take my own pulse. Living abroad has made me aware of quirks in myself and in other expatriate friends which we might not have found quirkish — or might have shed — if we had stayed in Ireland: gregariousness, restlessness, impulsiveness, readiness to feel guilt, eagerness to respond to a genuine appeal. Some of these are, I recognize, due to our nostalgia for old rural values which have faded now in Ireland too. They no longer work. The last time I honoured my mother's old Irish habit of entertaining tramps — she had regulars who used to come once a week for a meal — was fifteen years ago. I had taken part in a demonstration, marching on Downing Street in some good cause, and had while doing so struck up a conversation with a lonely Pakistani who confided that his social life consisted in attending all the demos in London. Stricken by the spectacle of such isolation, I invited him to Christmas dinner to the subsequent shock of both my American husband and a French house guest. The occasion was disastrous, for our guest was a vegetarian, unimpressed by Christmas — it had not occurred to me that his ethnicity might clash with mine — and did not get on with the others. Also, he misinterpreted my interest in him and expected the connection to be kept up. Mine had been the sort of impulsive foolishness which English writers, as long ago as Jane Austen, used instructively to deride. My only excuse for it is that the shift in Irish society together with my own moving away from that society had left my certitudes in a state of flux.

After that, I gave up my nostalgia for rural values. Ethnic fade set in — though, in way, I was shrewdly true to my thrifty heritage in that I got a short story out of the episode. I turned it to good use.

Another quirk: we — well some of us — think in spirals rather than in linear progressions. I think it was the Irish Australian, Thomas Keneally, who noted this or something like it not long ago. But I knew already. I am writing this piece spirally, starting in the middle, then adding bits to the beginning and end, wrapping and winding my thoughts around each other the way certain insects build their nests. Celtic traceries spiral too, and I am awaiting the day when someone discovers that the spiral is stored in chemical form in our brain and genetically passed on. Perhaps by coincidence, our history too has been cyclic. 'Our categories of feeling,' writes Denis Donoghue, 'have been flagrantly limited; our history has been at once intense and monotonous.'

Yes: patterns repeated themselves and, culturally, we were for a long time cut off. We were people of the edge, the periphery, the old ways. The Romans never reached us and neither did the Industrial Revolution. Neither did anything like the French Revolution take place in Ireland nor — until now — were we able to free ourselves from a peculiarly authoritarian form of Catholicism. Anti-clericalism spurted briefly a century ago at the time of Parnell, and again during the Irish Civil War of 1922 when hard-liners were excommunicated by certain bishops. But these were quickly damped fires. That great surge of fury which the French and the Mexicans and other Catholic peoples wreaked on their oppressive priests was never given free reign in Ireland. Anger was held in or turned, incestuously, on ourselves. Surely our sly, sudden rages go back to that? And our flexibility when we get abroad where, blessedly, the pressures are off and there can be an almost Platonic joy in completing our own narrow experience by the discovery of cultural models with more scope. Despite the cynical gibes, it is *not* just for the money that Ireland joined the EU. Europe provides a cultural framework in which many of us feel happily at home. Joyce's glee at recognising in anti-imperialist Trieste an experience close to the Irish one has had many parallels. Even without them, the sheer variousness of the European arena provides a mental liberation, and the discovery, for example, that Roman Catholic culture is more subtle than the sample we were given can be exciting. Ours was long regarded as a mission country, and we got the authoritarian version for simple souls which the Church doled out to those who knew no better than to accept it. I am talking of the past. We always do. Like our twilights, it takes longer than elsewhere to fade.

> *For the great Gaels of Ireland*
> *are the men that God made mad,*

The Imagination as Battlefield

For all their wars are merry.
And all their songs are sad.

G K Chesterton

The madness had method.

Nationalist songs and fictions make war by other means. If you lose a war, they can still promote an image of your aims and prowess which may, in the long run, do you more good than a few passing victories. The tactic must be as old as Homer, and a prolonged use of it not only turned us into a litigious people but directed our litigiousness towards the domain of words. (We are, for instance, remarkably quick to take libel actions, with the result that our writers have always had to be wary of being sued, a risk about which I, as a writer's child, learned almost as early as I did about traffic accidents and chimney-fires. Libel threats were the likelier danger in our family. My father, who ran a magazine for some years, had to contend with several, and, much later, my own first novel had to be withdrawn because of one.)

The imagination, you see, is taken seriously in Ireland. As proof of this, consider the history of censorship. Introduced in 1929, it remained draconian until the 1960's when it began gradually to fade. Consider too the sponsorship of the arts which succeeded it, the fact that writers living in Ireland pay no taxes on what they earn from their writing and that some receive an income from the state. Both censoring and sponsoring — putting aside their respective merits — show concern for the power of words.

That we should have been alert to this power is hardly surprising in view of our ancient poverty. Words cost less to produce than the other arts and had, in the past, to make up for the lack of them. For a long time our culture, like a broken mosaic, had great pale patches onto which we projected verbal accounts of our missing heritage. Our folk tales are full of fantasies about brightly lit buildings rising by night from the bog, and Gaelic poetry has a special category of 'vision poems'. Now that other arts flourish in Ireland, most notably that of film, Irish visions can and are being projected fully on screen. This is good news. But the phenomenon is recent. For a long time verbal descriptions stood in for the more costly arts in much the way that those terse messages do which you see on museum walls whence paintings have for some reason been removed: 'on loan', 'being restored', 'stolen', 'absent', 'never produced'.

This thought was borne in on me during a recent trip to Sicily, another much-colonised island, all of whose invaders — Greeks, Romans, Arabs, Normans, Spaniards — left behind swaggering stone testimony to their dominance: valleys full of temples, acres of dazzling mosaics, soaring and serpentine baroque churches. In Ireland, the English left us no legacy fit either to compare with Bourbon grandeur or to make up for what the native Celts might perhaps have built if left alone.

The stories of magic palaces suggest that we felt the lack, and I, as the daughter of two wistful patriots, spent much of my early childhood tramping through brambly fields in search of Celtic remains. These were usually a few sad stones buried under nettles, often only half excavated and always in need of the verbal gloss and encomium which my parents would eagerly supply.

Our cultural heritage, you see, was half dream, and the dream mixed memory with desire. It also faked the chronicle as other ethnic groups have done to soothe their pride.

In our case, though, the dream was so efficiently harnessed to our political aims that they became braided together and words became empowered.

Literary imaginations are apt to be aggressive at the best of times and ours always had a lot to be aggressive about. Our notorious 'Celtic hyperbole' was a distortion designed to outface other distortions. 'No,' is often a writer's starting point, 'No, it wasn't — isn't — like that.

The Imagination as Battlefield

Let me explain.' Then the one with the pen — or personal computer — starts a fashion such as 'revisionist' history or 'history from below', promotes 'marginal' or ethnic values or provides a fantasy to console or stimulate potential readers.

To be sure, such impulses are not peculiar to Ireland. Oscillating between evasion and agitprop, fantasy colours most lives. Aggression is one of its guises and it can hollow out a counter-fantasy by parody, as a terrorist might an edifice or a mouse a cheese. James Joyce's and Flann O'Brien's mock-epics are examples. In comfortable countries, though, fantasy is more apt to concern itself with individual hopes.

Consider, for example, the students in my Los Angeles karate class.

I worked out with them, off and on, for ten years by the end of which we were all black belts: fitter but no younger which, in the beguiling climate of LA, we had half expected to be. This bonding delusion made us forbearing with each other, which was just as well since we were a volatile mix. Southern California attracts dreamers and, during our years together, one member of our group ran a scam which landed him in gaol; two came to grief in a bar-room fight; another, hoping to become a martial arts movie star, paid a plastic surgeon to break and remake his jaw; and our instructor told us soberly of his plans to live forever. He calculated that a breakthrough in the research into DNA must fairly soon crack the code which programmes us all to die — whereupon the coded message could be reversed. When that happened he, thanks to his healthy lifestyle, hoped to be still here and in good enough physical shape to benefit. He would become immortal — in the flesh! — having rumbled Nature's scam, secularised the Christian dream and given up all immediate pleasures in the hope of getting them back a hundredfold. His diets were draconian; he exercised for several hours every day, and wrote away for special health-giving drugs. An ex-Mormon, he clearly conceived of the terrestrial paradise as likely to be restored in Los Angeles County.

They were optimists, you see! Dreamers on a grand scale! Admirers of the knock-out blow, they would have been baffled to learn that Irish nationalist myth had managed to turn defeat into a source of pride. Their own dreams were individual ones, so they were courteously tolerant and, as good Americans, respectful of one another's right to pursue personal happiness, each in his own way.

The contrast with Irish imaginings is interesting since, despite the totally different values, much of the raw dream material is the same. For instance, the idea that a magic drug exists: the 'water of life', which can confer immortality, occurs in Irish folklore, and the recycling of the Christian story for immediate purposes was precisely what the Irish patriot-poet, Padraig Pearse, did in the early years of this century when he prophesied that he, like Christ, would die to free his people. Astonishingly, this somewhat blasphemous prophecy was realised when, in 1916, he and a pathetically small force of Irish nationalists took to the streets.

In the beginning was the Word.

Yes, but in most cases its promise remains barren. When for instance, one enraged motorist shouts at another, 'I'll kill you, you bastard,' he is indulging in symbolic action and letting words — with a small 'w' — stand in for the act. But in Irish experience battles fought in the arena of the imagination led to actual gain. Pearse's words thus acquired the authority of the biblical Word. His fantasy then froze into a reality as hard to remove as the one *it* had helped overthrow. A secular religion was born

Historians marvel at the confusion, muddle and crazy bravery which, erupting in the Easter Rising of 1916, sparked off the Irish nationalist conflagration and led, five years later, to independence. The mix was surreal, as the French surrealist, Raymond Queneau, must have

The Imagination as Battlefield

recognised, for he wrote a novel — *Sally Meara* — about it. But the reality was odder than his novel.

Attempting a sober explanation, the historian, F. S. L. Lyons, writes '... the key to understanding is to keep constantly in mind that preparations proceeded at two distinct levels. We have to deal not only with a secret movement (indeed, with a secret movement within a secret movement), but also with an open movement which, unknown to its leader, was being penetrated by the secret movement.' Enough! the mind flinches. Unsurprisingly, to quote another sober historian, J. J. Lee, the Rising 'went off at half cock'. No wonder more basic forms of cock and penetration turn up in *Sally Meara*.

The story of 1916 is one of too many cooks falling into a broth wherein some perished and whence others — as in Celtic folk tales about magic cauldrons — emerged empowered. All acquired stature, and both the survivors and the dead were now ungainsayable, as Yeats's famous poem makes clear.

> *O but we talked at large before*
> *The sixteen men were shot,*
> *But who can talk of give and take,*
> *What should be and what not*
> *While those dead men are loitering there*
> *To stir the boiling pot?*

'In the event,' writes J. J. Lee, 'the Rising had turned into a blood sacrifice. But it had not been planned that way from the outset.'

Maybe not, but bloody poetic prophecies had prepared it. Three of the prophetic poets were among the seven signatories to the Declaration of Independence and were executed by the British along with other leaders. Three out of seven is a surprisingly high ratio of poets to warriors. No wonder things went off at half cock. And no wonder either that the participants were able, resourcefully, to turn their descent into the streets into a sort of miracle play and, having read their Declaration of Independence to a few astonished loiterers, to validate it by their deaths. Poets have their own cunning, and Yeats's admission that their deaths changed his mind about their cause testifies to the manipulativeness of their imaginative legacy. He himself then took up where they left off, became one of the new set of scriptwriters and helped change other minds too. He subsequently worried whether his words had sent more men out to die. Conor Cruise O'Brien later claimed that they had indeed done so and that he was right to worry and, later still, O'Brien himself was attacked for opposing the recent nationalist fight in the North. Tom Paulin, for instance, has accused him of thereby supporting 'a permanent Unionist state'. Such arguments seem eternal.

Words become flesh easily in Ireland and can have the force of a curse or prayer. It is hard to forget how, back in 1916, speeches validated by 'the blood of the martyrs' helped rouse not only the country but also American-Irish sympathies which then played a role in achieving independence. Now, once again, the peace-talks in Northern Ireland have American-Irish sponsorship: more cyclic experience..

Long after independence, the Irish imagination was to go on being a battleground. The agitprop, which had been used to mobilise the people against England, then mobilised one faction against another. The nationalist myth was fissile. First it gave rise to Civil War. Then, over the coming decades, 'God and the dead generations', invoked at the start of the Declaration of Independence, would be used by the new native rulers to curb the personal independence of those living on the island at any one time. The people, according to De Valera, had no right to do wrong. They were part of a larger, mystic Ireland which owed it to God and the dead to live with heroic virtue. Censorship and coercive laws outlawing divorce, contraception and other freedoms ensured until very recently that people who stayed in Ireland had little choice about this.

But not everyone did stay. Jobs were scarce. Emigration kept up a steady flow. Four out of five children born between 1931 and 1941 — my own generation — left. I find, reading the literature on the subject, that this exodus was regarded (by, for instance, *The Irish Banking Review* in 1958) as 'a useful safety valve' and I do see why. Without it, there might well have been unrest and the coercive nationalist myth might have been challenged more effectively than it was. As things were, its only challenge came from sour and helpless jokes — though these were as often turned on private as on public targets.

Irish mockery balances Irish myth-making, and the courteous acceptance of other people's follies which I admired in California could no more thrive in Dublin's climate than could a jacaranda tree. In Dublin, personal dreams of any magnitude are grist to the satirist's mill, and magazines like *Phoenix* are adept at deflation. Sceptical laughter has always been an Irish pleasure for, after all, if you cannot have your heart's desire, the next best thing is to laugh at the overweening fellow who thinks he can. Many of our most successful writers specialised in a needling derision of their society's more soft-headed delusions. Think of Swift, Merriman, Wilde, Shaw and Flann O'Brien.

At its best, as in Swift's *A Modest Proposal* — the proposal was that the hungry poor be encouraged to eat their children — the satire sprang from an altruistic indignation with social injustice. More often, as Yeats perceived, it arose from envy and the 'great hatred, little room' of a country unable to employ its young.

To take a more technical approach: bitter wit benefits from keeping jokes in pickle which is only possible in smallish cities like Dublin or Florence. Dante drew on the Florentine pickle jar in his day. In mine — I spent some years in Florence in the '60s — the communal pickling jar was once again well-stocked with vintage anecdotes. Dublin wit too can be preserved for decades without losing its sting. In both cities the gibes are *ad hominem*. Victims are named. This is rare in a big metropolis. Here are two jokes from the Irish pickle jar. The first, now fifty years old, described Dublin's two leading theatres — one of which specialised in homosexual actors, the other in peasant plays — as 'Sodom and Begorrah'. The second is fresher. It calls condoms 'just in Casies', after Bishop Casey of Galway who, having failed to use one, was found to be instead using diocesan funds to mollify the mother of his secret son.

Oral jokes are uncensorable and are a useful antidote to a surfeit of rhetoric. Spiteful or not, the oral tradition had many uses during the years when censorship had a stranglehold on the written one — a hold which it has not quite let go. According to journalist Kevin Myers, writing in a recent number of the *Spectator*, 'Throughout the 1980s, the Church could still command the state to back its ban on condoms, even while Aids was spreading throughout Ireland. Not merely was abortion banned, so too was information about it — even *Private Eye* appeared in special Irish editions with advertisements for condoms and abortion clinics removed.'

This last whimper of censorship reminds me of its heyday, when my father, Sean, was acknowledged to be its most persistent critic. He could afford to be outspoken because his books were published in London and New York. They were, however, banned in Ireland, as were those of most Irish writers as well as major literary works by almost everyone else. Ireland, the most obedient of Catholic countries, applied criteria tougher than the Vatican's.

Though a child then, I was aware of belonging to a pariah family, for we lived in a village where everyone knew everyone and where, during the 1940s, nobody had motorcars and everyone took the bus. On days when the

The Imagination as Battlefield

passengers on our local number 59 turned their heads away and pretended not to see us, I knew that Sean had 'done it again'. He had attacked some pillar of the Establishment, 'let down the country in front of foreigners', or, worse, criticised the Church. This was dangerous in those years. On one occasion a predecessor of Bishop Casey's, in the See of Galway, began to sue Sean, who, on being advised by lawyers that he would be broken if he resisted, had to apologise.

Off the bus and discreetly out of sight, well-wishers sometimes cheered him on. 'Keep up the good fight,' they'd whisper, 'we'd be with you if we could' and then slink nervously away. Jobs were few, precarious and often in the gift of the Church.

Now, a half century later, the battle for free speech has been won — though bear in mind that divorce has only just been legalised in Ireland, and abortion is still illegal. By and large, though, as my father's parish priest observed at his memorial service in 1991, the breed of inquisitorial churchmen Sean fought against 'is now an endangered species'. They have become even more endangered since, as a result of the spate of scandals which an unmuzzled press has recently been able to reveal about paedophile priests. Desperate to put its own house in order, the Irish Catholic church is on the defensive. Television and the freeing up of frontiers have defeated old clerical efforts to keep a wall around the Irish imaginative world. Anger at those old oppressive methods explains the glee with which Irish journalists now show up the priests who have been charged with sodomising little boys. Kevin Myers quotes a new joke: 'What do Catholic priests hand round after dinner?' Answer: 'The Under-Eights.'

Impatience with pretensions, delusions and rhetoric seems to have escalated of recent years and there is a healthy irreverence in much of the writing coming out of Ireland. *Saeva indignatio* razors through the novels of — for instance — Patrick McCabe and Michael Collins, and

I relished the humour in a story by Michael O'Loughlin about some Irish workers in Germany who are so incensed by a German sympathiser's request for contributions 'to the (Irish) people's liberation struggle' that they pelt him with beer cans. Well-meaning German bystanders — this is happening at an Irish folk-music event — taking them for Englishmen, then attack them, and one Irish lad gets stabbed. Slogans like 'the people's liberation struggle' must ring hollowly in the ears of men whose fatherland can offer them no jobs.

There are great numbers of immigrant Irish workers in my part of North London. Many are old men who wear softened old suits the way the poor in Ireland always used to do. Jack Yeats painted men like them: tattered and formal with dancing coat tails. They are not the 'dead generations' but a cohort of ghosts who left years ago and now live on British welfare cheques. Sometimes, to cheer themselves up, they sing a scrap of an Irish song. They are probably too demoralised to throw their beer cans at anyone who, as in O'Loughlin's story, asked for contributions to the 'waging of the people's liberation struggle'.

Bitterer and more likely to throw a beer can are some over-qualified, articulate, younger men who work here as carpenters, window-cleaners and the like: men who go back and forth to the Republic, are at home neither here nor there and feel, surely rightly, that they should be able to get better jobs. They read more books than their English peers do, and their conversation is livelier. Some write. Words matter to them and they complain about the lack of good chat here in London. The traditional Ireland to which they sometimes return — West Cork and Kerry for example — has a nostalgic pull but is surely as unreal now as a theme park or set of theme parks if it cannot employ its own population.

It produced people to whose warmth and solidarity I can testify, for five years ago when my parents became ill, then

The Imagination as Battlefield

unable to cope, their Dublin neighbours rallied and helped as generously as if they had been relatives — more kindly, indeed, than many relatives. I was then living half in London, half in California and couldn't always get back fast enough in a crisis. But the tribal virtues of old Ireland — the kindest neighbour was a woman from Kerry — shone through in a way which explains why we expatriates are so ready to be taken in by our own half-true, half-self-deceiving memories — and why we are then so often enraged by ourselves for yielding to their beguiling charm. Our imaginative life is a battle between siren feeling and the effort to see clearly in circumstances which are often as confusingly blurred as the spirals on bronze-age Celtic stones.

'The phrase "Romantic Ireland",' writes Denis Donoghue, 'denotes an idea or a sentiment, and mostly the sentiment of desire or loss.' Later, he concludes that it is 'a set of values espoused, promoted, bought and sold ... endlessly deconstructed, and yet even now, not entirely annulled.' Yes.

Seamus Heaney's verse, which is firmly anchored in particularity, captures the precise feel of those memories which would lure me back — but might then disappoint. In his verse there is no disappointment. Read this:

> *And here is love*
> *like a tinsmith's scoop*
> *sunk past its gleam*
> *in the meal-bin.*

I remembered the verse at random, but memory is shrewd. There is no rhetoric here, so no need for the satiric, balancing, defensive joke. He lifts precision to a level of universal, reconciling truth. His is the voice of *l'imaginaire irlandais* at its self-transcending best.

Imagining Conamara

Bob Quinn

I was driving from Galway to Foxford, Co. Mayo two years ago with my neighbour, poet and playwright Johnny Cóil Mhaidhc and as is my custom in Mayo I got lost. After many side roads, turns and returns to the pilgrimage town of Knock which has some kind of magnetic attraction for lost souls we finally got back on the right road. Johnny turned to me and said 'Má's oileán beag fhéin í Éireann, is tír an-mhór í.' For a small island, Ireland is a very big country.

Unless you are a journalist or tourist, i.e., trading in clichés, it is sensible to accept and celebrate the extraordinary detail of this country. Every generalisation about the place can be simultaneously true and false.

Yes, we have great hatred, little room; but being human are capable of much charity.

Yes, we are xenophobic but strangers usually experience a warm welcome.

Yes, we are at base illiterate peasants but we have produced one of the great literatures in Europe and, after Latin and Greek, the oldest. And that's apart from writers in the English language!

Yes, we were (may still be) a broken people but we were the first to achieve independence from Empire.

Yes, we are anti-intellectual but we are presently the most generous country in the world towards individual artists.

How can the observer resolve these contradictions?

One approach might be to try to imaginatively reconstruct the humanity of one's own village, street or apartment block and from that microcosm deduce the nature of the larger world. The extraordinary variety of opinions and personalities that can live within affective distance of each other is always a salutary sample of the variety of the world. One should, and usually does, base one's *weltanschaung* on the local. You are as likely to be an inch as a mile from an accurate universal perception — but you will certainly be closer than those villains who categorise us all as A, B, or C for advertising purposes.

Thus I choose to imagine Ireland as it is and as it might be through the prism of a part of it in which I have lived for the past twenty-five years — a period which, happily for the purposes of these words, roughly coincides with one of the greatest periods of social change that have ever hit this small island.

Where I live was a century ago a place of thatched cottages, donkey transport, subsistence living and poverty. Electricity preceded me to this village by only ten years. The area is called Conamara. It is described as a Gaeltacht or Irish-speaking community and it is located in the West of Ireland.

However, the donkey is now obsolete.

Conamara is now, for good or ill, alive with pubs, discos, Walkmen, microwaves, TVs, National Lottery mania, traffic jams every day in summer, after Mass every Sunday and at 3 o'clock every weekday when parents pick up their children from school.

About thirty miles away is the county town called Galway which is officially a city and reputed to be the Athens of Ireland but I can't vouch for it, being only an occasional visitor there. Galway city has not sufficient symphony orchestras, art galleries, schools of music, museums, corps de ballet or opera companies to attract me regularly.

Come to think of it, it does not possess even one of these amenities. Instead it has recently had an explosion of hotels and apartment blocks. And tourists.

The place in which I live is utterly rural and not sufficiently pacified to attract package tours.

Twenty-five years ago I decided to leave Ireland. I'd had enough. I wanted to emigrate again, take the Bád Bán finally, get away from the claustrophobic religiosity and worse, the Anglo-American serfdom of my birthplace, my culture, my country. I thought of New York, San Francisco, Nova Scotia, Montreal, Munich, Teheran, Paris, Moscow, London, Leeds and all of the places I had known in my itinerant life. None of them looked vaguely like an improvement on Ireland, bad as it was, so I decided to emigrate inland.

An interior émigré?

Sort of. I became an immigrant in my own country, to this place, Conamara. At least here the Irish language, Gaelic, was everyday speech and might constitute, I hoped, a linguistic bulwark against the worst excesses of Coca-Cola speak or even the pretentious London and New York-aping nonsense that passed as respectable social and literary criticism in this country (it still does).

That was 1970.

A quarter of a century later I am still here in Conamara, which is due to a peculiar combination of the Force of Inertia and the fact that I still can't think of a better place to live.

In my first few years here I became increasingly irritated by the image the outside world had of the place: painters and tourists had described it as a wilderness of lakes and bogs and mountains and big mountainy men and little fresh faced colleens and Paul Henry landscapes and poitín makers and dole men.

It was a patently false image.

But it was analogous to the expectations that the French and Germans and Americans had of the larger island, Ireland itself. This was good for tourism but was more a product of the adman's necrophiliac imagination, the tourist's memories and the Dubliner's weekend fantasies than anything approaching reality.

I found South Conamara to be full of people who didn't read *The Irish Times* but knew Boston and London intimately, who weren't obsessed with 'the media', had no interest in the gossip from Dublin 4 but knew their local politicians' every move as intimately as they knew every rock and field around them, the forty ways to cut turf, the lines of a boat, their neighbours' business, the weather in the sky. They also knew how to work the system.

They were and are the largest bilingual community on the island; they were as much at home on the sea as on the land and their popular music was a weird unaccompanied singing which bore more resemblance to a mullah's call to prayer than to the Beatles. They knew nothing of European classical music. Initially I thought they had no sense of rhythm; they found it hard to carry a 3:4 beat when they occasionally strayed into country and western. On the other hand, I found the internal rhythms and nuances of their own singing utterly alien to my Chopin/Bach/Debussy background.

They were as different from the denizens of Dublin as Orangemen are. But the Pale would never and probably never will acknowledge this. Conamara people are as alien and as alienated from pan-celticism as the abandoned working class suburbs of Dublin.

Overcoming my own urban cultural egocentricity took a long time.

You recall the early imaginings of a child?

It thinks it can't possibly have sprung from those awful people, its parents. It must have been born of kind, generous, non-authoritarian Princes.

Well, I began to project such imaginings onto Conamara and its people. They couldn't possibly fit into the narrow, puritanical, timid, suburban island of the Ireland I knew. A parish priest I met confided in me that his parishioners weren't like 'us'; they were more like pagans, he said. This cheered me up greatly. The late Patrick Lindsay said he had retired to Conamara because there was a touch of savagery there which he found amenable. He came from Belmullet, Co. Mayo.

I once said to a friend in Conamara that she wasn't civilised. She was highly insulted until I explained that I meant she was not city-reared and therefore hadn't a strait-jacketed mind like me. It was my kind of compliment but I doubt if she has yet forgiven me.

What is the point?

Freedom, that's what. However much these people might be constrained by living in small, almost tribal circumstances, their behaviour displayed a freedom of action and independence of mind, not to mention an initiative, that I was not accustomed to. For a start, they were more widely travelled than any comparable group on this island. As a community they knew Boston, Chicago, London and Huddersfield more intimately than Dublin — possibly even than Galway. They didn't emigrate. They simply went to their extended family: uncles, aunts, older brothers and sisters, grannies and grandads who had carved out a space for them amidst alien corn. They constituted a sharply etched diaspora within the larger diaspora of general Irish emigration.

They had, and still have, that most rare commodity — a sense of who they were. Good, bad or indifferent, it might be based on intermarriage, on hundreds of uncles and aunts and brothers and sisters and cousins scattered from Carna to Camden town; it might smack of tribalism, but it undoubtedly had and still has a sense of community.

This tribalism or sense of family is a bit like presently unfashionable nationalism. You dismiss its reality and power at your peril and as ineffectually as if you outlawed sin.

This sense of community did not mean that Conamara people didn't squabble. I have seen men trying to tear the heads off each other one night; next day I have observed the combatants chatting amiably at a bar counter. I have heard of a man returning to a pub 13 years after he was bounced out of it, to seek redress. There might be inter-familial tensions, based on wrongs of a hundred years ago, there might be the occasional eruption when drink was taken, but they still lived close to each other, still walked the same roads, went to the same funerals and weddings and sailed in the same races.

Why?

Because they knew that, whatever the slings and arrows from outside, however the politicians and development authorities might want to organise their lives, no matter how much money the EU might pour in, when the billion was eventually squandered, whenever the last cobweb factory closed they were still stuck on the same patch, were still going to have to rely on one another. *Ar scáth a chéile a mhaireann's na ndaoine.* People live in each other's shadows.

If I was giving a sermon I would say there was a moral there somewhere for the rest of the tribes on this island.

However, I want to talk about the Royal House into which I imagined my neighbours all those years ago. It was wilful, I know. I wanted to distance them from what I perceived as the awfulness of Ireland. Just as the celtophiles in the 19th century imagined the general population of the island to be descendants of so-called Celts, to distinguish them from mother England, I looked for clues, things that distinguished Conamara people from their imposed post-famine romantic image, and at the same time linked them with other places and people.

If you look hard enough you'll find evidence for any hypothesis.

I found plenty of evidence: Sean-Nós singing, styles of boat building, linguistic affinities, local customs, maritime traditions, related stories.

The result was three films and a book called *Atlantean, Ireland's North African and Maritime Heritage*.

These suggested that we owed as much to the various Mediterranean cultures, be they Coptic or Islamic or Berber, as we did to our cold northern neighbours, including the Vikings. My findings were treated with silence by academics, with contempt by some traditionalists and with delight by intellectual anarchists.

The most positive reaction was from a brave historian in UCG who said to me it was the single most important intellectual event in 20 years in this country. On the other hand a famous female Irish language poetess described it as a compendium of nonsense.

But the real reward was more interesting. You know the story of Jacob's folly? The one about the lazy farmer who won't lift a finger and just dreams of winning the lottery? In a dream one night an angel tells him there is treasure buried under one of his apple trees. He has 200 trees. So he begins to dig around the roots of the trees and after much toil and sweat finds — nothing. Disgusted, the farmer retreats to his bed. But the following Autumn he has the best crop of apples in the region and makes a fortune selling them.

The treasure I found from my apple trees was a personal perception of Ireland which makes it to me the most interesting place on earth.

Firstly, it is an island with a deeply indented coastline. This makes it a paradise not just for drug smugglers. Historically, an endless insular coastline means it has been open to every influence under the sun, be it Gallic tribes, Barbary pirates, Vikings, Normans, Tudors, Arab whalers,

Huguenots, Palatines, Italian postmen, Welsh mercenaries, Scottish Gallowglasses, Megalithic argonauts, seeds from the Caribbean, American Ph.D's and multi-nationals, German fence-erectors, Coptic Monks, Quaker do-gooders, Roman missionaries, Spanish Armadas, Russian trawlers. The island is like a circle, a defined enclosure with an infinity of external contacts.

As John de Courcy Ireland put it:

'An té a mbíonn long aige, geibheann sé cóir. He who has a boat will get a breeze. A proverbial statement like that does not emanate from a landlubberly people. Long before the Irish language, or a Celtic language of any description came into this country of ours, we were a maritime people, and the blood that flows in every one of us here, every one of us in the country, is blood that came across the sea. I do not accept that because we have a reputation for holiness in this country, that our ancestors were dropped from Heaven. And you can go back to the very earliest moment in history and you find that the first people who came into our country came by sea, and they laid the foundations of a maritime tradition that this country has, richer and older than almost any country in Europe.'

Probably an unfortunate modern analogy would be Sky TV. You can't stop it. It becomes, for good or ill — usually for ill — part of what we are. So every visitor — invader if you like — has contributed to the make up of this island population. It is not a melting pot, though. Only huge empires can aspire to such an anti-human homogeneity. We are a compendium of tribes.

I first got that perception in Conamara and I found it very liberating. It lifted a veil from this island, made it seem less narrow or cut-off, more varied and interesting. It meant that we were not some tiny, homogenous bunch of Celtic Catholic Gaeilgeoirs bravely and irrelevantly surviving on the periphery of Godless Western Europe. This was how customarily we presented ourselves officially to ourselves.

But neither were we a nation of poets, saints and scholars, irritable Joyceans, urbane Wildeans, mad Beckettians or hairy Yeatsians in every street and pub. We were neither Celtic aristocrats nor secondhand Britons. We were in fact, a healthy mongrel race. Now, if it's a choice between mongrel and thoroughbred, well, give me the mongrel every time. They are not robber barons and they don't interbreed to the point of insanity.

So I have imagined, like Yeat's Fisherman, a construct of Ireland which enables me to continue living here, a place of infinite variety of temperature and temperament. When one expression of our beliefs temporarily depresses me (such as our adoption of the 'free market' mentality) I lean on another equally temporary but presently attractive trait (our belief that we are undergoing an artistic renaissance).

Thus my affection for this island and its people exactly counterpoints our weather. Very changeable. Its personality is amenable to a million constructions. That makes life interesting.

Now here's the bad news.

We're losing our infinite variety, the endless array of personality and idiosyncrasy that has made this island interesting to not just me. Like the Catholic Church we are losing our mystery.

Listen to children in any village in Ireland and you will notice a peculiar thing: they are losing their regional accents. This is more noticeable of course with middle-class children. That has always been their parents' ambition. But it is now happening to children from less prosperous strata. Their voices and accents are converging in a kind of TV cartoonspeak. This is a good thing, you might say; it breaks down regional barriers, minimises their perception of others as strange and threatening, gives all children a common language.

The trouble is, the dialect is imposed. It is a kind of vox Americana, and it is the linguistic environment which, thanks to TV and the cinema, most Irish people now inhabit.

Having English as the majority language accelerates the process in Ireland. The potential for this was a trickle thirty years ago when 'Irish' television first hit this island. Now it has become a torrent.

Among teenagers and yuppies one of its variants has been clearly identified as the DART accent — referring to the prosperous South Dublin area served by the Rapid Transit system. Some call it the furstenburg accent, referring to an upmarket beer whose appalling taste was overcome by an expensive advertising campaign.

Is an accent shift so important?

I think so. It indicates a move away from something, a move towards something else. It is away from the indigenous; towards the cosmopolitan. Away from the rooted; towards the transient. Away from the local; towards the distant green hills. Away from self-confidence; towards a sense of shame.

It is a rejection of the dreary familiar. In this sense it is Joycean. In this sense teenagers are Joycean, even though they know nothing of him. As Joyce (like the early Abbey Theatre) could not have indulged his hedonism without the patronage of romantic maiden ladies, neither can our teenagers indulge their rejection without the romanticism of Brussels which pays their education fees or the utopianism of TV soap operas which provide them with new self-images, new dialects.

Adults are undergoing the same transformation.

Their rejection expresses itself in this accent shift. Is this so significant? I believe so.

I imagine it to be analogous to the unprecedented language shift that happened in this island after the Great Famine. The shift from Irish to English. That shift was based on more than words, words, words. It betokened a final collapse of faith in the physical land and the culture that had nurtured the people for millennia. Mass hunger and death will encourage people to examine their basic premises. The land was basic and was found wanting. The Irish language was rooted in it. It had to be jettisoned too. Into the cultural vacuum poured organised religion, a continental Jansenism purporting to be Catholicism. (Now that Catholicism is also being jettisoned here, what will pour into that vacuum?)

Is this a fair comparison? Too dramatic? Juxtaposing a fairly superficial shift in the way a language is spoken with the wholesale abandonment of a language itself? All we can do is try to grasp straws in the wind, to find out what is happening to us, what is bewildering us, why are we frightened?

Because we are frightened.

Frightened of what?

Of drugs, rave parties, joyriding, mugging, housebreaking, rapes, child abuse, consumerism, unemployment, high-level corruption, tabloid journalism, all of the ills we see on TV which signal our emergence as a modern western state, a member of the rich man's club.

All of the ills that are making us cower behind locked doors and BMWs, smoke alarms, community alert schemes and calls for more law and order. Fortress Ireland is emerging. We are suffering from the Westerner's disease of information obesity: we know instantly and intimately what's wrong, can describe it in detail but like the eunuchs in Don Juan's Hell, are increasingly rendered incapable of action by the rain of facts that deepen the drought of the will.

One of the great ironies of Ireland today is the number of well-heeled foreigners who are buying property (and passports) here on the assumption that this is a simple, Catholic, unspoiled, slightly backward country in which they and their children will be safe from the social excesses contingent on their own triumphant capitalism. Little do they know that they are inadvertently helping to transform their chosen haven into just another dangerous part of the world.

This amuses me. Perversely it reminds me of the behaviour of some Conamara people when they enter powerful enclaves. In 1987 I made a series of films on my émigré neighbours' existence in London. I found many chameleons who had adapted to their new circumstances, had adopted English accents, condemned IRA outrages in tabloid-speak, became invisible to the watchdogs of the Prevention of Terrorism Act. By contrast, and much more attractive, were a group called the flytippers among whom were some of my neighbours' children. These young people lived in the cracks, the interstices, the gaps in respectable society.

They were people who had assessed the situation in London as precisely as Indian immigrants to Mexico City, the ones who knew within weeks precisely how much public officials need to be bribed to achieve anything.

My ex-neighbours saw instantly that Mrs Thatcher's building programme in inner London required a more efficient building rubble disposal system than the London public authority was capable of providing. They moved into the breach.

Dumping sites were inadequate. They were also thirty miles from central London. The flytippers immediately grasped the solution. They hired lorries, collected the rubble from Mrs. Thatcher's Tory friends' development sites and promptly dumped it, more efficiently in gardens, on quiet streets, in basements, outside Wormwood Scrubbs prison, all under the eyes of respectable, law-abiding citizens in central London. They were enacting the logic of capitalism: you can do anything as long as you are not caught.

The were mini-multi-nationals. Some were caught. They laughed at the fines. The rewards enabled them to do so. A few were caught and did time. They became cleverer. So it goes.

I am torn between condemning their lack of a sense of 'civics' and admiration for their daring. On balance I think positively of them: they were faced with a hostile culture, the adoptive culture of their own rulers; they were following in the footsteps of their navvying parents who had come to London without any English and suffered ignominy as a result; the flytippers were wary of social entrapment.

All of these stray thoughts are stimulated by Conamara.

Lest I be accused of romanticising this place and its people I should say that I am writing this in the grim afterbirth of Christmas, on a cold and wet January night. There is a gale battering the house. The nearest cinema is thirty miles away. My newly planted trees are leafless, defenceless. The phone is kaput. Soon the electricity will go. I could venture a mile to the pub where I will find only a handful of men brooding into their pints. Every winter it is the same. I confess that every winter for the past twenty years I have sworn that I will leave in March. But something stops me.

For instance, recently there was an 'Airneáin' — a song and story session — in the pub: my own son was among the musicians, and I am still warmed by the occasion. There is some kind of unwritten law in the best of these sessions — at least in this area — that causes people to behave, to become sensitive to unspoken rules of attention, respect, sensibility. It might have been something as simple as the absence of amplification — no large black and threatening loudspeakers which make small talk impossible, force normally quiet people to shout. Here the musicians — Johnny Conghaile leading three melodeons, two flutes, a fiddle and the respectful bodhran — had only their subtlety to capture attention in a crowded hostelry.

And they did. Even the inevitable bodhran — which is usually recommended to be played with a penknife — was kept muffled by its owner so that it would not dominate. Middle-aged people, unable to resist the complex rhythms, broke into little self-conscious dances; grown men held hands and sang long songs. An 86-year-old began to formally recite a story which went on for half-an-hour. It was from the 2000-year-old Fianna epic. He was given the compliment of total silence. A stray, out-of-season German said she had never experienced anything like it.

As usual, in the middle of it, I realised that such occasions were the reason I have endured here so long.

I store up these to leaven the occasional bleakness such as tonight and to think how such events may, for all I know, be repeated all over this island — although I doubt it.

I am reminded of the Swedish attitude to America: 'To hell with the United States, I want to go back to Minnesota'. In the same spirit, you can keep the concept 'Ireland'. I prefer the concept 'Conamara'. And I hope every man and woman from the Shankill Road to Andersonstown, from Killarney to Dublin 4, from Bagenalstown to Buncrana and every other locality in this island which has pride in itself thinks the same.

It is the only answer to the *vox Americana* — or the *vox Bruxelliana* for that matter.

Language, Stories, Healing

Angela Bourke

I grew up in Dublin, speaking only English, but Irish was there around the edges. 'An bhfuil na leabaí réidh?' my father used to ask my mother in the evening, when my sisters and I were small: 'Are the beds ready?' I didn't know then, and I don't suppose he ever knew, that the plural of *leaba*, bed, is not *leabaí* but *leapacha*. He had grown up in Foxford, Co. Mayo, an old garrison town whose people prided themselves on their good English and felt little in common with the Irish-speakers who still lived in the surrounding countryside. My mother's Irish was better, but at her national school in Co. Cavan, just across the road from the farm where she grew up, she had been taught a northern dialect which few people in Dublin understood. Dad used his smattering of Irish to communicate with her in code, and start the process of putting us to bed without alerting us. She answered him in English, and it worked for a while.

At school, Irish was compulsory — and confusing. What did it mean, to call this set of unfamiliar sounds and meanings Irish? We lived in Ireland; we were Irish. England was elsewhere, the other. So surely the language we spoke all day should be called Irish? Learning it was easy, though, with endless repetition; and sometimes it was fun. Like learning to dance, it was a series of clever tricks; paces I could be put through. It was rhymes and spellings and tables to chant in comforting unison; a special language for that place: 'Dún an doras,' 'Close the door,' 'Téigí a chodladh,' 'All go to sleep.' Fifty children put their heads down on their folded arms and pretended to be asleep. Nothing that happened in Irish was real. We learned about the work of the blacksmith, haymaking, a day on the bog, and our schoolbooks were full of rural images. Where we lived there were no donkeys or turf-bogs, and no potato-fields, although a woman who lived near us did keep hens. We played in a concrete-paved lane behind our row of red-brick houses, and hit tennis balls against the peeling paint of garage doors, or lost them in the nettles. We were three miles from the centre of Dublin, but farmers drove flocks of sheep down from the mountains along our main road, and the local butchers drove cattle up the same road to their slaughterhouses.

Like my parents, our teachers had grown up in small towns or in the country, and still pined for things rural, or at least presented themselves to children as doing so. They showed us Dublin as a hostile place, makeshift and artificial, where we would always have to be on our guard. Products of De Valera's Ireland, they warned us about the corruptions of the modern world, embodied in everything that came from England. Religion and Irish were to be talismans against all that.

At home there was no talk of ideology, but my parents loved the country. Reserved, shy and apolitical, my father was much moved by the romantic nationalism which endowed landscapes of grass and mountain and water with mystery and meaning, and denied the reality of the urban. He chafed at the difficulty of maintaining a family in Dublin, in lower-middle-class respectability, and remembered his own childhood as a time of walking and cycling the country roads around Foxford, fishing the River Moy and rowing on Loughs Conn and Cullen. His accent changed when he pronounced those place names: became rounder and fuller as he seemed to taste the word 'Lough' on his tongue.

My mother made bread every day, marmalade from Seville oranges every January, jam every summer. She walked briskly and enjoyed fresh air. She didn't want to talk about her childhood. Memories were quickly dismissed. All our grandparents were dead, and I was hungry for stories.

Sometimes on Sundays our family went out for picnics, to the seaside, or the mountains. Sitting on a rug beside the big reservoir, Dad told us about the valley that had been flooded to store water for the city, and explained that its name, Poulaphouca, *Poll an Phúca*, meant 'the Púca's water-hole.' The Púca was a sort of boogey-man, he told us, who lived around there somewhere. We were eating sandwiches, our backs to some blackberry bushes, and I can still see their curving, prickly branches against the blue sky as I looked back over my shoulder, fascinated and terrified. Poulaphouca had been a valley where people lived and farmed. Now it was lost and gone forever, overwhelmed by the wateriness of its name, but the mysterious *Púca* still haunted it. Or maybe I have invented those blackberry bushes. We did pick blackberries for jam in late summer every year, but much later, studying folklore, I learned that though the *Púca* is man-shaped in my father's native Mayo, in other parts of the country it is a sort of horse, which fouls the blackberries every year at Hallowe'en, making them unfit to eat.

Words and names in Irish were doorways into stories. Ardee in County Louth was Áth Fhirdia: the place where the hero Cú Chulainn killed his boyhood companion Ferdia in single combat at the ford. Kildare was Cill Dara, the oak church built by St Brigid in the sixth century. These stories were in our school reading books, which I read from cover to cover as soon as I got them. Children's books were scarce. Whenever I was sick in winter, I spent the days in my parents' bedroom. My mother brought me hot drinks and clean handkerchiefs — old, soft worn ones that had been my father's — and I spread my colouring books and jigsaw across the double bed. Left alone, I used to explore the bookcase, full of fly-blown hardbacks that no-one ever read, and copies of *Hobbies Weekly,* bound and covered in wallpaper by my father. I read the plans for model aeroplanes and wooden toys; I read *David Copperfield* twice, and James Thurber's *The White Deer* many times. I read incomprehensible novels on thick spongy paper in the uniform hardback covers of the Book Club, and then I found *The Golden Legends of the Gael,* by Maud Joynt, and I read and read and reread it.

It was printed on cheap wartime paper, already brittle and yellow when I was seven. I wrote my name on it, my address and my age, and when its cover came off I mended it with the bright blue sticky tape that Dad had brought home from somewhere.

The Golden Legends of the Gael was just as good as Grimm's *Fairy Tales,* with shape-changing, colour and magic, love, sorrow, and battles; but it was about Ireland: about kings and queens, poets and warriors who lived here long ago, and it told the stories with a wealth of vivid detail that our school readers sadly lacked. Much later I learned that Maud Joynt had been a celticist, a contemporary of William Butler Yeats, and that the stories I had read were scholarly translations of mediaeval manuscript sagas.

One of them told about Nuada, a king who lost an arm in battle. The physician, Dian Cécht, made him an artificial arm of silver, which could imitate the movements of a real one, and from it he was known as Nuada Silverarm. But Miach and Airmed, son and daughter of Dian Cécht, were even more skilled than their father. They could tell by the smoke that rose from a house whether anyone was sick within, and what remedy was needed. Miach found the severed arm and reconnected it, using the words of a special healing charm, but this made his father so insanely jealous that he murdered him. From his grave grew 365 herbs, one for every joint and sinew of his body, and Airmed collected them and arranged them on her cloak according to their healing properties. Again, jealousy made Dian Cécht violent, and he scattered the herbs. The text adds that this is the reason nobody now knows the virtues of plants, unless the Holy Spirit has taught them.

Lost and gone forever: the knowledge of herbs; the farms of Poulaphouca; the heroes of old. The elegiac tone was everywhere. Or maybe I was listening out for it. Eldest of my family, living in an old house, with few other children as neighbours, I lived a lot in books, and acquired a taste for gloom quite early.

The story of Airmed and Miach had said that Airmed's knowledge was lost. The only way to learn things now was to be taught by the Holy Spirit. Many of those Old Irish tales take that attitude: written by monks, they are ambivalent about the pre-Christian traditions they relate. Their message is hard on girls and women: it makes us troublemakers, irrelevant, defeated. The Holy Spirit was on the side of men, of schools and churches. 'Unless a man be born again,' our catechism told us, 'of water and the Holy Ghost, he shall not enter into the Kingdom of Heaven.' So it was not enough to be born of woman. Born a girl, you had no chance at all.

Outside school and that book of *Golden Legends*, the written word dealt almost exclusively with England. The Enid Blyton mysteries and boarding-school books we borrowed from the library were set there, and so were the comics: the *Bunty* and the *Judy*, the *Beano* and the *Dandy*. Nowhere in them were children taught by nuns, as we were. Nowhere was Ireland or Irish mentioned. Instead children learned French, from teachers called Ma'm'selle; they drank ginger beer; they met the vicar, and the vicar's wife, and helmet-wearing policemen called P.C. Something-or-other. No priests, no Gardaí, no changing baby brother's nappies, no going to mass, no first communion, no going to the toilet. Instead there were owls hooting, and hedgehogs drinking saucers of milk, and girls learning ballet and grooming ponies.

Stories set in Ireland were few and far between, and invariably rural. To be properly Irish, it seemed, you should be barefoot, poor, and pious, and preferably the child of a widow. The short stories of Patrick Pearse were all about such children, and when we read some of them in Irish in our last year of primary school, it seemed that where we lived was a frighteningly narrow place. On one side was England, a collage of godless, sooty factories, great houses and impossibly snobbish boarding schools; but rural Ireland was equally exotic: sunlit and numinous, green and blackberried, forgiving and pure. The further west one went, the purer it got, apparently, so that the Conamara Gaeltacht of Pearse's stories was a place where being good was easy, and love was everywhere. I wanted to go there.

A year after starting secondary school, I spent a month in Conamara, at Irish College, and found that nobody was barefoot. This was not after all the simple romantic life of Pearse's stories, but it did have another kind of magic.

We stayed in the dormitories of a boarding school and attended classes in Irish every morning, learning vocabulary and some grammar by memorising songs and stories, blessings and curses. In the afternoons we walked in straggling gangs to swim at a beach two or three miles away, constructing elaborate friendships and flirtations as we went, and wearing holes in our thin summer shoes. In the evenings we dressed up, in our own or each other's clothes, put on what makeup we could find, and walked again, to the hall in the village for a nightly céilí. Every summer as a teenager I went back to Irish College. We were away from our parents; away from the rigid decorum of our single-sex schools; away from paved streets and brick walls and the disapproving eyes of adults. The teachers who supervised us were young, and mostly male, and they were on holiday too. Like us, they played ball games, and swam and sang and danced, and when thirteen- and fifteen-year-olds fell in love, as they did every year, and went everywhere hand-in-hand, they usually smiled.

That combination of fresh air, sunshine, and adolescent sexuality was inseparable from the air that smelled of seaweed and turf-smoke and the shadows the little flat-bottomed clouds cast on the landscape of green and brown and blue; and its language was Irish. Back at school in Dublin, the Irish-language syllabus was as boring as ever — pallid and pedestrian by comparison with English and History — but pronouncing its complicated consonants and seductive diphthongs the Conamara way, I could imagine myself back in a world of stone walls, beaches and grass, long songs sung unaccompanied, place names packed with stories, and adults who let us dance till we were red in the face and drenched in sweat, instead of treating us as children or nuisances.

Nostalgia for summer hooked neatly into the earlier escapism of the *Golden Legends of the Gael*. The cold Holy Spirit androgyny which school seemed to require as a corollary of cleverness contrasted strongly with the frank acceptance in the Gaeltacht that a female body could house a mind. The resourceful Airmed with her cloakful of healing herbs seemed more at home there than in Dublin.

The rigid polarisation of my imagined environment into materialistic Dublin and spiritual Gaeltacht didn't survive the sixties. About the time I started university, new violence in Northern Ireland was helping to discredit the romantic nationalism I had grown up with. I was doing Celtic Studies with a few like-minded souls, but other people our age who rejected the authoritarianism of their schooling were turning firmly away from Irish tradition as they immersed themselves in left-wing politics.

We loved our subject: revelled in the study of early Irish, picking texts apart as though with scalpels; but often we found ourselves typecast as owlish, irrelevant and reactionary. At parties people would hear the word 'Irish' and grow glassy-eyed, visibly making assumptions about

Language, Stories, Healing

my politics, social attitudes and religious beliefs. For a long time too, any identification with Irish was suspect, at home and abroad. Friends whose passports showed their names in Irish were detained at British ports for days and nights without explanation or apology.

Revisionism threw out quite a few healthy cultural babies with the ideological bath water. Most painfully for me, feminism and an interest in Irish appeared to be mutually exclusive. The majority of the women who were doing such exciting work in challenging the authoritarian structures of our society didn't want to know about Irish. They associated it with the most repressive and fatalistic aspects of our culture. Almost axiomatically, the Gaeltacht, so often invoked by patriarchal nationalists, symbolised all the forces that had kept women subservient to men.

Peig Sayers, the Kerry storyteller and verbal artist whose autobiography had been on the school curriculum for generations, became a joke. Invariably photographed wearing a shawl, she was resoundingly rejected as a role model for modern women. Her independence, her strength, wit and insight, might almost never have been. Airmed, spreading her cloak and arranging the healing herbs upon it, was never mentioned.

Jumping through the hoops of scholarship, I resigned myself to this division. On one side I kept the rigorous study of language; meticulous reading of texts; on the other side were my identification with women, my own sense of self. But it is not possible to stay divided like that, and as I grow older, I find myself less and less willing to separate the things I believe in from the things I know. My love of stories makes a sort of bridge, heals the rift. I work on traditions about women and girls: I read the oral poetry and stories of the Irish language, listening for the voices of real women. I write fiction that tries to make an insistent account of individual experience sound through the neutral, laconic narratives of folktale, or through the registers of English spoken unselfconsciously in Ireland.

We have urgent need of stories in Ireland at the moment, as our society comes to terms with painful memories. All at once, it seems, we are trying to cope with the famine of the mid-nineteenth century, when a million people died of fever or starvation and another million emigrated; with 25 years of violence in Northern Ireland, followed by the sudden possibility of peace, and then more violence; and with a heartbreaking series of revelations about betrayal of trust, about domestic violence, and about cruelties secretly inflicted on women and children. The old narratives will no longer serve, and it is not just politicians and journalists who are struggling to make sense of it all. Religion used to offer answers and explanations, but more and more it is artists who confront the broken certainties that lie all around. The literature and oral tradition of the Irish language were used for so long in the service of self-righteous patriarchal nationalism that for years the most creative and radical minds in the country wanted nothing to do with them, but that is changing. Film-makers, painters and poets are finding ways of expressing what was done and what was felt, using the threads of what we already had, but could no longer see. More and more, as silenced voices speak, the need for different kinds of language is being acknowledged.

Irish is a language that was almost lost. A hundred years ago, children were sent to school with tally-sticks on strings around their necks. Every time a child spoke Irish, her stick was marked with a notch by teacher or parent, and punishment was doled out accordingly. In this century, memories of that pain persist. Some revivalists expressed their love of the Irish language and its literature as contempt for English; some teachers enforced its study with just as much cruelty as had been used to stamp it out. Many of those whose vision of the world was broader retaliated by repudiating everything Gaelic.

For a hundred years after the famine, Irish people behaved as though they could afford only one language; as though they had to choose between Irish and English: material poverty translated into cultural frugality. One book I read as a child told how a fox whose leg was caught in a trap would gnaw off its own foot in order to be free. The cruelty perpetrated in the name of language on the children who wore tally-sticks was that sort of desperate measure: a grim hacking off of part of the cultural body: a self-mutilation designed to end a greater pain.

'All our wars were merry, and all our songs were sad,' said Brendan Behan, and indeed there is no shortage of sentimentality in what passes for Irish oral tradition. But alongside and underneath the facile expression of sadness runs an idiom that knows about the experience of pain; and about living through and overcoming it rather than wallowing in it. In my own work I come back again and again to one story. It was told in Irish in 1938 by a master storyteller, Éamon a Búrc from Conamara, recorded and written down by a professional folklore collector, preserved in an archive, and published in a scholarly edition more than forty years later.[1]

A Young Woman Taken By The Fairies

Long ago here in Conamara there was a couple who married. They had two sons and a daughter: two fine men; and no woman in the country was more beautiful than the girl when she grew up. One day, one of the young men went out to the hill to cut a load of heather, and as he set about cutting, he noticed some very fine stuff growing on a cliff. Up he went to the top, cutting away, when suddenly a voice said out of the cliff, 'What are you doing there?'

'Cutting heather,' said the young man.

'I'm telling you,' said the thing in the cliff — the person — 'you'd better leave it, if you know what's good for you!'

He stopped cutting. But on his way home with the load on his back he tripped, and a woman's voice spoke behind him:

'You've not heard the last of this, you know. We're not finished with you by any means. You've let the rain in on us from every side and left us in a terrible state.'

He threw down his load and ran, leaving it there. He came home and told his story. When his father and mother heard what had happened, they said he had had no business staying in that place once he heard the first voice.

'I left the load behind,' he said, 'right where I fell, where the woman spoke to me.'

'Well, then,' said the father and mother, 'leave it there!'

And he did; they never moved it.

Well and good. They had cows out on the hill, and every morning they used to go out to milk them, the sons taking turns. Then one day they were both away from home on some business, something they had to do one day. And the day was growing late, evening was falling, and the father told the young woman to go out and milk the cows. She didn't want to. She said it was getting late.

'Hurry up,' said the mother. 'Don't let it get any later.'

The sun was still fairly high. She took her can and her naggin measure — that's what they used in those days — and out she went. The place she came to was a sort of marsh, boggy marginal land, with the cows standing on the side of a grassy little hill in the middle. She put down the can, left it there and set off, milking the cows into the naggin. Whenever the naggin was full she would carry it over and pour it into the tin can. She went on like that, naggin by naggin, until the can was full: a great big can full to the top with milk.

She turned around to drive the cows ahead of her, and suddenly she couldn't see the can; she had no idea where in God's name she was. She kept stumbling; evening was coming; the day had darkened up with fog, and if she was there till now she couldn't find the can, or the naggin, from the moment she left it out of her hand. She went on until night fell, falling and stumbling in the black darkness among hills and mountains and bogs, and going up to her waist in rivers, with no idea where in God's name she was, until she saw a light in the distance:

'I declare to goodness,' she said, 'that must be someone's house. I'd be better to head there than die here, for certainly if I keep walking like this, taking the knocks I'm taking, and wet to the skin as I am, there'll be no life left in me by morning.'

She made for the house where she saw the light, barely able to move her legs one in front of the other, her clothes were so wet and so full of mud. When she entered the house, she saw people moving around, and food and drink on a table set in the middle of the floor; a red-haired woman serving the food, and a black-haired woman by her side. But as soon as the black-haired woman saw the young woman approaching, she came to the door and told her not to eat any food whatsoever that might be offered to her until she herself divided it and gave it to her:

'For the sake of all you ever saw or ever will see, don't you taste a bite of the food the red-haired woman is serving till I come and tell you to eat. You can eat then and it will do you no harm.'

When the young woman entered the house she was called by her own name and surname and made heartily welcome. And it wasn't long before a fine woman like a queen came in from the other room, a beautiful woman, and she too made her welcome and ordered the red-haired woman to set out a supper for this woman who had just come in. The red-haired woman set to work. But while the food was being prepared, the black-haired woman quietly shook her head to tell her she shouldn't go to the table or eat anything. The red-haired woman laid out the food and told her to sit down. She said she wasn't hungry, that she wouldn't eat anything until morning.

'That's very strange behaviour,' said this red-haired woman. 'Eat. It's good for you. Everyone knows that a person who's been walking since morning needs food by now.'

'I don't,' said the earthly woman, 'I can't eat anything.'

The mistress came in again — the mistress of the fairy-fort, for that's where she was — and told the woman to set out food for her.

'I've already set it out for her,' said the red-haired woman, 'but she wouldn't eat.'

'Set it out for her again until she eats,' said a big fat woman who had come in from the other room. 'My instructions. Tell her she has to eat it.'

The red-haired woman set food out for her, but she said she wouldn't eat it; she wasn't hungry and she couldn't possibly eat.

'You may as well eat,' said the red-haired woman. 'Talking won't do any good. You have to eat; it's sinful for a person to fast when there's so much food and drink here for anyone who wants it.'

'I don't want it, thank you very much and long life to you,' said the earthly woman.

The red-haired woman kept at her for a while after that, trying to persuade her to eat.

'No,' the young woman kept saying, 'I can't.'

And every time the red-haired woman ordered the earthly woman to eat, the dark-haired woman would pass through the other side of the house and shake her head, telling her not to. Finally, when she still wouldn't eat, the red-haired woman gave up:

'Maybe if Bríd set out food for her she'd eat.' — Bríd was the dark-haired woman.

'Set out food for her,' said the Queen of the fairy fort, putting her head out the door of the other room. 'You, Bríd.'

Bríd got up and set food and drink before her. She ate then, and when she had eaten she felt better. But Bríd — the woman they called Bríd — whispered to her as she sat at the table:

'For the sake of all you ever saw or ever will see, don't taste any bite in this place but what I set in front of you, for if you do you'll never be able to leave.'

Well and good. The next day the same thing happened. The red-haired woman set out food for her but she wouldn't eat. And when the next day came and she didn't come home to her family, they went to the hill to look for her, but found no sign of her. All that night and all the next day her two brothers searched. They found the can full of milk on the patch of grass on the bog, with the naggin laid down beside it. Of course they took the milk home, I suppose, though they hadn't much interest in it, they were so upset about their sister. They didn't know where in the name of God she'd gone. Six days that week they searched for her, every day that she was missing, until they decided she must have done away with herself — thrown herself into a lake or river and drowned. There was no sign of her anywhere. But all the time she was held in the fairy fort. Six days and six nights, and they didn't stop or sleep all that time, day or night, but mourned and searched for her all over.

That went on until the sixth night. She was kept indoors, and while she was inside, Bríd — the woman they called Bríd in the fairy fort — was standing at the door. She saw a man approaching.

'Goodness,' she said, 'here's Seán Rua coming.'

And the earthly woman didn't know who Seán Rua was, but in he came. And who was he — he'd been dead a certain length of time — but a first cousin of her own! He came into the fairy fort and stood with his back to the fire looking at his first cousin who was being kept there.

'What brought you here?' he asked, taking her by the shoulder and shoving her towards the door.

She told him she didn't know.

'Get out right now,' he said, 'and go home.'

'She will not,' said the red-haired woman.

The Queen herself came out and told the young woman not to leave, but she said she would, and a fight broke out then between Seán Rua, with Bríd helping him, and those others. They were killing each other.

'We'd better send her home,' said the Queen.

They grabbed her and threw her out onto the ground. Seán Rua and Bríd went with her some distance from the house, until she was fairly close to her own home. But no sooner had Seán Rua and Bríd left her than she fell down right beside the house and a sharp spine, like a big needle, was driven into her knee. She kept walking, though her knee was very sore, and sure enough, she made it home. When she came in, she didn't mention it, but they asked what had happened to her, and blessed her and praised her and gave her butter and salt and every other sort of thing they could. She told them the story from start to finish and their conversation didn't touch on falls or injuries or anything of that kind from then until morning.

But when morning came there was a terrible pain in her knee, and by the next afternoon it was so bad she couldn't stand on the floor. By the third day she had to stay in bed altogether; they had to make up a bed for her by the fire; people had to nurse her, while she moaned and screamed — screeching at the top of her voice with pain.

The knee swelled. Doctors came to her. The priest came to her, trying to cure her. They tried everything: plasters and poultices and herbs, but nothing could be done for her, until she'd been there three months, and the leg had swollen so much and got so big no-one could lift it. It was swollen right up to the top of her thigh.

She spent almost a year lying on her back in bed, screaming all the time with pain. No-one could lay a finger on her, she screamed so much with pain and agony, until one night an old woman — an old beggar-woman — came in and sat by the fire.

'Is it any harm to ask what ails the woman who's screaming?' she asked.

'No harm at all,' said the mother of the young woman, and told her what I've told you: all that had happened to her, how she had been taken into the fairy fort and made her way home, and how she had gone out milking in the first place.

'Hm,' said the old woman.

'And the first thing she felt was when she fell down and something like a sharp spine went up into her knee and the knee swelled up. There's no cure for her, and I'm afraid there won't be until she dies.'

'If it was daylight,' said the old woman, 'I could do something. We'll have to wait till daylight.'

Next morning, as soon as day dawned, the old woman got up and went out before the sun was up, and whatever secret communication she had with herbs, she went out and the herb told her — she brought it in between two fingers — told her it would work.

'Now,' said the old woman, 'off you go to where the bonfire is'- it was around St John's Eve, so there was a bonfire in the village. She told them to go to the bonfire site and look for some trace of bone, even ashes, and to bring home some of the burnt embers from the fire:[2]

'And mix them with this herb here and put them on her knee between two cloths,' said the old woman. 'If that won't cure her, I don't know what will.'

The mother and the two brothers went out and did everything as the old woman had told them. The old woman had collected the herb for them, so they mixed up the bones that were burnt to ashes and embers from the bonfire with the herb, wrapped it in cloth, and laid it all between two cloths on her knee.

'Don't move that now,' said the old woman, 'until tomorrow morning. Whatever pain or torment she suffers until then, don't lay a finger on her, and I guarantee she'll be healed by morning as soon as the sun rises. Goodbye to you now,' she said, 'I'm leaving.'

'Oh,' said the woman of the house, 'you can't be.'

'I am,' she said. 'I'm not staying here any longer.'

She went out.

'You know,' said the father and the sons, 'you should give that old woman something.'

But when the woman of the house went out after her a few minutes later, to pay her something, she couldn't see her anywhere.

'I don't know where in the name of God she went,' she said.

But from the moment the plaster, or poultice, was put on the young woman's knee, there never was such horror under the sun as the pain she felt, or the way she screamed until day broke. They did as the old woman had said however. Before sunrise in the morning they went to her, and when they took away the rags and lifted off the plaster that morning, a needle as long as your finger, or longer, came out of her knee along with the cloth, for every man to see. From that moment on she improved. By the end of a week she could sit by the fire; at the end of a month she could move around the house, and after three months she was as well as she had ever been.

That's no lie. It happened here in Conamara in the old days.

The blessings of God and the Church on the souls of the dead, and may we and the company be seventeen hundred thousand times better a year from tonight!

❖ ❖ ❖ ❖ ❖

Perpetual Motion

Fintan O'Toole

In his memoir of growing up in the small American town of Piedmont, West Virginia, the black American writer Henry Louis Gates Jnr. remembers that the whole west side of the place, where the road rises towards the Allegheny Mountains, was called 'Arch Hill': 'I figured that it was called that because it was shaped like the arch of your foot. Twenty-five years later, I learned that what the coloured people called "Arch Hill" had all along been "Irish Hill". Cracked me up when Pop told me that.'[1]

The trick of the tongue that turned Irish into Arch, transforming the ethnic identity of the O'Rourkes, O'Briens, O'Reillys and O'Neills who lived there into the shape of a human footprint was a happy one. To hear in the word 'Irish' the shape of a foot in motion is to catch the true note of a culture that is not just marked but actually defined by the perpetual motion of the people who bear it. Emigration and exile, the journeys to and from home, are the very heartbeat of Irish culture. To imagine Ireland is to imagine a journey. And in the last few decades the ways of measuring the distances traversed in that journey have been changing.

When I was ten, we started to learn the metric system of measurement at school. Where before we had measured everything by British Imperial standards — walking for miles, drinking pints of milk, measuring out the goals for football on the basis that every large step was a yard — now we were to realise that there was a whole other system, neater, more logical, more redolent of the future.

Though we did not understand this at the time, the decision that we should learn about metres and litres was itself highly political, a symbol that we would no longer be ex-colonials, measuring out our days in imperial yards and shackled feet, but Europeans. Ireland was preparing to join the European Economic Community, and we were entranced with the idea that some great transformation was on the way. Once, part of my school homework was to measure in metres and centimetres the ordinary objects around the house: the height of the door, the width of the table, the depth of the kitchen sink. And even writing down their dimensions in this new language of a glossy, standard Europe, the objects themselves seemed transformed, no longer their mundane selves, but promising and full of allure.

For me, part of that allure was a simple but radiant image. We learned that the metre was a standard measure of distance, and that every metre we measured was a copy of a prototype metre-long metal bar held in the International Bureau of Weights and Measures in Paris. It was a nice thing to know. There was something comforting about feeling that every distance you could ever traverse was a version of the same distance, that every step you could take was in step with all the others around the world. That unseen, inscrutable length of platinum and iridium in a Parisian vault seemed to guarantee that something, at least, would always be exact and unchanging. Behind all the transformations of Ireland at the time, the epic shift from a traditional and rural society to a modern and urban one seemed to lie this new guarantee of continuity and certainty.

That comforting idea — that everything could change and still be continuous — was one way of imagining Ireland. And as I grew up, the metric system suggested another. It came from the fact that even after we had joined the European Economic Community and adopted the metric system, we all continued to ignore the

I am fascinated and moved by this depiction of a young woman's unhappiness: her ill-treatment by adults, her bewilderment and pain, her resistance expressed through rejection of food, and her final release through the wisdom of an older woman, a stranger to her family, who knows the virtues of herbs. I read it as metaphor for things that can occur in any age; in any society, whether rural or urban. It happens that the language of this story is Irish, and that its setting is Conamara: landscape of small lakes and hilly bogland. Its terms of reference, often trivialised and denigrated in literate culture, are familiar in Irish oral tradition: fairy people live near humans, hidden and unseen, often underground, and if they are offended, will seek revenge.[3] They abduct children and young women, sometimes leaving changelings in their place. Their world is seductive and rich, but illusory, and anyone who eats their food is lost to normal life forever.

Stories like these deal with ambivalence and paradox; with transitions in human life and situations that are beyond human control. Their protagonists stumble into a world where everything is other, and emerge either mutilated or enriched. Fairy legends like this one are meditations on change, reassuringly rooted in the past. Their association with intimately-known landscapes appeals to both credulity and memory, yet their psychology is timeless. Many, if not most, are about women and children.

For me, the compelling strangeness of this story and others like it is one of the rewards of knowing Irish. The vivid descriptions of a hidden world where the normal is turned inside out give access to a psychic and imaginative richness that is specially valuable because so little known. As Irish society painfully confronts an avalanche of revelations of child sex abuse, incest, and teenage pregnancies hidden and repudiated, stories like this can perhaps offer the possibility of healing.

FOOTNOTES

1. Told in Irish by Éamon a Búrc, Cill Chiaráin, Carna, Co. Galway, and recorded on Ediphone by Liam Mac Coisdeala, 29 September, 1938. Mac Coisdeala's transcription, entitled "Bean Óg a Tugadh sa mBruíon," is in the Irish Folklore Collection archive at University College Dublin (ms IFC 529: 304-317). Edited by Peadar Ó Ceannabháin in his *Éamon a Búrc: Scéalta*, (Dublin: An Clóchomhar, 1983) 267 - 73, it is here translated by Angela Bourke, by kind permission of Professor Bo Almqvist, for the IFC, and of the editor. See also my "Fairies and Anorexia: Nuala Ní Domhnaill's Amazing Grass," in P*roceedings of the Harvard Celtic Colloquium* XIII (1993) 25 - 38.

2. For magical uses of embers of a bonfire, compare Mary Carbery *The Farm by Lough Gur* (Cork: Mercier, 1937) 163.

3. For a discussion of fairy-belief in oral narrative as a vernacular cognitive system, see my essays "The Virtual Reality of Irish Fairy Legend" *Éire / Ireland* 31, 1 & 2 (Spring-Summer 1996) 7-25, and "Reading a Woman's Death: Colonial Text and Oral Tradition in 19th Century Ireland," in *Feminist Studies* 21, No 3 (Fall 1995) 553-586.

measurements and use the old ones. Even the Gaelic Athletic Association, the guardian of traditional Irish games like hurling and Gaelic football, converted yards to metres and started to call a 50, the free kick that you get when one of the opposing players puts the ball beyond his own end-line, a 45. But everyone went on thinking of it as a 50. To this day, we drink pints of beer, complain that the beach is miles away, ask for so many square yards of carpet. To this day, if I am told something in metric figures, I have to work out what it would be in imperial figures before it has any meaning to me. And that is a second way of imagining Ireland: that a culture is about the way people measure things, and that the residue of an old way of measuring hangs around long after it has ceased to have an official existence.

But there is a third way of imagining Ireland suggested by the metric system, and it struck me recently when I discovered the disturbing fact that the way of fixing the length of the metre has, after all, changed. The platinum and iridium bar may still be in Paris, but it is no longer the ultimate definition of distance. These days, distance is measured, quite literally, in time. Since 1983, length is measured by the clock, not the measuring-tape. a metre is no longer a version of a precious metal bar in Paris, but the distance that light travels in a given infinitesmal fraction of a second. The ultimate point of reference is no longer physically present, no longer fixed and immutable, but itself in frantic motion, a blur of light that covers 300 million metres a second. It is itself a journey.

These three lessons from the metric system each contain a truth about Ireland. It is a country in which change itself provides the only possible continuity. It is a culture whose way of measuring things are often unofficial, vestigial and inexplicit, even to insiders. And it is, above all, a country whose journeys can no longer be measured by fixed standards, but that have to be gauged by their relation to other, imaginative journeys.

Ireland, one of the world's great emigrant societies, has undergone a similar change in its way of measuring distance. It used to be that at all points around the globe, in Boston or in Glasgow, in New York or in London, in Sydney or in Berlin, the emigrant's distance could be measured in relation to a fixed, unchanging standard called Ireland. Somewhere beyond the waters, locked away in a sealed and sacred vault as an ultimate point of reference, there was a fixed, unchanging length of space, an island in the Atlantic standing firm against the waves and wind. Every step the traveller took could be, imaginatively at least, measured in distance to or from that remembered home.

An example is in Padraic O Conaire's *Deoraiocht (Exile)* published in 1910 as the first major novel in the Gaelic language. It is striking in itself that one of the first real literary expressions of the revival of the Gaelic language as part of the nationalist resurgence of the early 20th century centres, not on the recovery of a fixed place and a finished past, but on the tormented wanderings in Ireland and England of a displaced man who becomes a freak in a travelling circus. Even more striking, though, is the irony of the following passage, describing social gatherings in a part of London called Little Ireland:

'There would be a man there who could relate the contents of Keating's *History of Ireland* ... And if somebody were to disagree with anything the savant said, he would just go to the big trunk he had brought with him from Ireland and take out a parcel wrapped in linen. He would open the parcel and take out a large book in manuscript. And how careful he was of that book. He would then show you in black and white where you had been wrong. And when he closed the book to put it away he would look at you as if to say "Now what have you to say for yourself?" But he never said a word.' [2]

O'Conaire's image of this man with his linen-wrapped parcel of unarguable history brought from Ireland into

Ireland as a place back east. And the political divisions of the island add to this disorientation. The most northerly part of the island is in 'the South', because it is part of the Republic. Places far to the south of it are in the North because they are in Northern Ireland.

Such confusions can be given coherence only by the imagination. There is, of course, a profound connection for all cultures between nationality and the fictive imagination. All national borders are, at a fundamental level, works of fiction. They separate the nation from all that is not the nation. And what they enclose is not just a physical space, but also the imaginative one. Nations are the product of history rather than geography, of culture rather than race. Like a book or play, they are made up. The nation has to be invented or written. While it is being written, everyone knows that it could be written otherwise. But when it has been written — in the form of laws and constitutions, of proclamations and declarations — the act of writing must be forgotten, transformed instead into the act of reading a pre-given past.

The conflict between writing the nation and reading it lies at the heart of Irish culture in the 20th century. It is an insoluble conflict because it arises from the most difficult contradiction of Irish politics and economics — the contradiction between places and people, between the search for a fixed national space and the existence of an unfixed, mobile population. Considered as a place, Ireland is a pre-given space, standing sharply out from the ocean that surrounds it. But considered as a people, Ireland is an unbounded sprawl, an incoherent network of memories and resentments, dreams and desperations, moving between the island itself and its diaspora in Britain, the United States, Australia, Canada and elsewhere.

The geographical Ireland, the bounded island, is a place that can be read. It can be imagined, albeit problematically, as the result of a given past, as the present form of an innate and immemorial Irishness. The second, exile is a perfect example of how Ireland imagined itself in the period of national revolt that led to the foundation of the Irish state in 1922. The old man's history book was the cultural equivalent of the metre bar in Paris, the token of a pre-given past against which everything could be measured. Everything was either authentic or inauthentic, either Irish or not-Irish. Samuel Beckett once answered an interviewer who asked him 'Vous êtes Anglais, Monsieur Beckett?' with a laconic 'Au contraire'. His joke contained a commentary on the way Irish identity had actually been constructed as a mere opposition to all things English. The fact that O'Conaire's old Irishman was actually living in England was occluded by the struggle to hang on to a fixed, finished identity. Where history and geography are confused and displaced by emigration, the appeal to the authority of an invented past becomes coercive. In the Little Irelands of the Irish imagination, there was for a long time an overwhelming temptation to read Ireland as a closed book rather than to imagine it as a blank page waiting to be written.

Yet in reality, the Irish imagination was formed by the instability of the place, by the fact that the people and the place were not the same thing. Most of the descendants of the people who lived in Ireland in the middle of the nineteenth century now live, not in Ireland, but in America, Britain, Australia and all other points of the globe. Emigration has been the overwhelming fact of Irish life for the last 150 years. And because of it, simple ideas of history and geography do not make sense. How can you have a linear history of a country when most of your ancestors' descendants live in other countries and belong to other histories? How can you have a simple geography when it is impossible even for the points of the compass to remain stable. For Ireland a sense of direction is difficult. Most Europeans think of it the far west, the edge of their continent. But most Irish-Americans, who make up the majority of those whose ethnic identity is Irish, think of demographic Ireland is a nation that cannot be read but must be written. And because it must be written, it could be written otherwise. Existing as it does, imaginatively, it is always open to the possibility of being re- imagined. As such, it poses a constant threat to the first Ireland. It questions its readings by remembering that they, too, were once written, that they are inventions, that they represent not an innate expression of the nation, but merely the one strand from a range of possibilities that happened to develop within the frame of the island of Ireland.

The great German critic Walter Benjamin reminds us that there are two kinds of storytellers, embodied, respectively, in the tiller of the soil and the trading seaman. The first carries 'the lore of the past, as it best reveals itself to natives of a place.' The second is imbued with 'the lore of faraway places, such as a much-travelled man brings home.' [3] Storytelling, Benjamin says, is most potent when it comes from 'the most intimate interpretation of these two archaic types.' Sometimes, at its most powerful — as in for instance the work of James Joyce — Irish culture combines the lore of the past and the lore of faraway places. But more often the two have been in contest with each other.

Modern Irish writing comes out of the attempt of the Irish Literary Revival to posit Ireland as a culture that could be read, and read through the lore of the past. The whole idea of a revival presupposes a belief that there is some intact inheritance from the past which can be recovered by careful reading. By clearing away the false impositions of Britishness and urban modernity, the lines of a culture implicit in the island itself could be deciphered and their meaning restored. Thus, William Butler Yeats, for instance, claimed that the modern Irish drama would be founded on a mediaeval poetic, and that he could track any authentic folk expression still in use back to classical times.

This was, of course, untrue. The revival was a writing that pretended to be a reading, an act of invention that pretended to be an act of restoration. The fact of emigration, the fact that the immediate past of the revival period was one of extraordinary dispersion was glossed over in the revival's emphasis on the authenticity of place. By taking place rather than people as the touchstone of Irishness, the revival was able to appeal to a sense of continuity and stability that were simply unavailable in contemporary Irish experience. But this effort involved an inevitable strain.

The strain lay in blotting out the fact that the need to imagine in Irish culture comes from emptiness and nostalgia — the emptiness felt by those left behind, on the one hand, and the nostalgia felt by those who left, on the other. Liam O'Flaherty's stark, grief-stricken story, *Going Into Exile*, written around the time the state was founded, is a good example of the first category. In it you can feel how the ebbing away of human reality in the act of emigration opens up a blank space to be filled by the imagination. There is an American Wake in progress, a ritual of mourning to mark the move to Boston the following day of a son and a daughter, Michael and Mary. O'Flaherty writes it like the Last Supper, a feast that is also a sombre preparation for a death. As the morning of departure dawns, the unseen, the unreal, the imagined takes a subtle grip: 'The stars were growing dim. A long way off invisible sparrows were chirping in their ivied perch in some distant hill or other ... Cocks crew, blackbirds carolled, a dog let loose from a cabin by an early riser chased madly after an imaginary robber, barking as if his tail were on fire. The people said goodbye and began to stream forth from Feeney's cabin.'[4]

Eventually, at the end of the story, the mother is left in a world of desolate imaginings, 'listening foolishly for an answering cry', imagining she can 'hear the crags simmering under the hot rays of the sun. It was something in her head that was singing.' This counterpoint between an emptying house and the tightening grip of the imaginary (the invisible sparrow, the imaginary robber, the simmering crags, the singing in the head) is emblematic of modern Irish culture. Reading between the lines, discerning meaning in the empty spaces, is often the task in hand.

A later O'Flaherty story, *The Letter*, virtually a follow-up to *Going into Exile*, can stand as a metaphor for this task. A peasant family is working in the fields. Their eldest daughter, Mary, has gone to America. They have had no letter from her for a long time, though a neighbour has written to say that Mary is without work. The family's two youngest daughters arrive home from school with a letter they have received from the postman. It is from Mary. The father opens it and takes out a cheque for twenty pounds, enough to buy a new horse to replace the one that died a year before. There is unbounded joy. Then the eldest son reads the letter aloud.

' "Dear Parents", the son began. "Oh mother, I am so lonely." It's all covered with blots same as if she were crying on the paper. "Daddy why did I ... why did I ever ..." It's hard to make it out ...yes ... "why did I ever come to this awful place? Say a prayer for me every night, mother. Your loving daughter Mary." ' [5]

After a long silence, the whole family begins to wail and weep. Nothing has been said, nothing made explicit. There is no explanation for the twenty pound cheque or for the daughter's anguish. But the family fills in the blanks. Reading between the lines and making out the tear-blotched letters, they imagine an unthinkable truth. Their reading of the letter is also a kind of writing, an engagement of their creative imaginations that gives shape and meaning to the barely discernible realities that the letters on the page hint at. This is what a culture defined by emigration does — it writes itself as it reads itself.

The paradox of the second category of Irish imagination, that of nostalgia for home on the part of those who have left is that *home* itself comes into focus only when one is away from home. Home is much more than a name we give to a dwelling place. It is also a whole set of connections and affections, the web of mutual recognition that we spin around ourselves and that gives us a place in the world. Older languages tend to contain this idea within themselves. In Gaelic, the terms *sa mbaile* and *sa bhaile* the equivalents of the English *at home* or the French *chez-soi*, are never used in the narrow sense of home as a dwelling. They imply, instead, that wider sense of a place in the world, a feeling of belonging that is buried deep within the word's meaning. That deeper meaning, the one that we employ when we say not merely that we are *at home* but that we *feel* at home is what Irish culture seems to seek.

Art, of course, has always drawn our attention to the connection between the narrow meaning of home as a place to live and the wider resonance of the word as a feeling of having a place in the world. But in the Irish imagination that connection belongs to life as well as to art. The Irish historian David Fitzpatrick, studying letters from Irish emigrants to Australia a century ago, noted how, for them, 'contemplation of "home" provided a vocabulary for the expression of emotional attachment and the exploration of personal identity.'[6]

It is particularly true of Irish culture that the imagination itself is inextricable from the idea of home, usually made powerful by the act of leaving it. The counterpoint in O'Flaherty's *Going into Exile* between an emptying house and the tightening grip of the imaginary is art, but it is also life. Looking at the emigrants' letters, David Fitzpatrick found that *home* had much more than a literal meaning, often 'evoking an alternative world of recollection and imagination'. In the network of recollection and imagination — remembering the past and inventing the future — that makes a culture, there's no place like home.

Emigration gave to Irish culture a particularly sharp realisation of the fact that a home is much more than a house. In his survey of 111 letters to and from Irish emigrants to Australia in the second half of the nineteenth century, Fitzpatrick found the word *home* 229 times, on average more than twice in each letter. One woman writing from Queensland used the term 30 times in three letters. And significantly the word was used far more often by the exiles than by those who remained in Ireland. Eighty one per cent of the uses were in letters from Australia, just 19 per cent in letters from Ireland.

In most cases, *home* was not used to refer to a house, but to a whole social world. Fitzpatrick lists the shades of meanings in these letters: a dwelling place, a household, a neighbourhood, a country, an unspecified place, an address, a place with special characteristics, a place with special emotional associations, a place to return to. 'Home', he found, 'was not only a symbol of shelter and comfort, but also a scene of sociability and matchmaking.' Yet, when the emigrants talked of 'home' in Australia, these larger associations were mostly absent. Adjectives suggesting warmth, comfort or sociability tended not to be used. *Home* came to mean just a household, 'typically used as part of a mundane dichotomy with school, shop or work-place.'[7]

Home became, in Irish culture, a place as much imagined as remembered or experienced. 'Home in Ireland', writes Fitzpatrick of the emigrants' letters, 'was both a real and an imagined location. As an economic unit it continued to affect the fortunes of Irish Australians through the transfer of money and gifts as well as the organisation of further movement. As an imagined location, it sometimes took the form of a dwelling, but equally often of a household or neighbourhood buzzing with banter and gossip. As a symbol of comfort, stability and usually affection, it provided an important source of solace for those facing the taxing and insecure life of the emigrant.'[8]

This imagined, symbolic home became, when it was re-imported into Ireland, the touchstone of both politics and religion. And it is also the link between politics and religion, the thread that bound Catholicism and nationalism, Protestantism and unionism, together. Because the idea of a homeland was so steeped in emotion and yearning, it came to be identified with a spiritual home, a land of milk and honey, a paradise both earthly and unearthly. Both Irish traditions — the Gaelic and Catholic one and the British and Protestant one — came to believe that only by making their home territory spiritually pure, dominated by the righteous believers in their own religion, could it be a fitting symbol on earth of the holy homeland in their heads. And thus a yearning that began as nostalgia has ended, in our own time, as bloody conflict. The roots of the feeling, in exile, in the act of going out into the world and living with people of different races and languages and traditions, were forgotten. A way of writing, of inventing and of imagining became a way of reading, of imposing, of defending. The job of culture is to make it into a way of writing again, and, appropriately, it is writers who have been searching for ways to do this.

That search has been encouraged by the fact that the basic distinction on which nostalgia relies — the distinction between home and abroad — has been falling apart. That old polarity is impossible in recent Irish writing, where the feeling in O'Flaherty's *Going into Exile* that the emigrant and the Ireland left behind are two worlds as separate as death and life has been replaced by a strong sense of Ireland itself as a place forever on the move between different worlds. In Sebastian Barry's recent play, *Prayers of Sherkin,* the central character, a young woman living on Sherkin Island off the south coast of, but touching on an image that serves for the bigger island of Ireland, asks her brother 'Do you not feel that this island is moored only lightly to the sea-bed, and might be off for the Americas at any moment?"[9]

Such a question arises from the profound social changes in Ireland that began in the 1960s and are still in progress. The impulse to emigration remains, of course, largely economic, and the surge of the late 1980s clearly followed from the 1979 oil crisis and the huge rise in unemployment. Economic underdevelopment and the failure to provide work for a growing population is not the wrong answer to the question of why it continues, but it is, since the 1960s, an insufficient answer. Belgium and Britain, for example, also had very high unemployment at the same time, but there was no British or Belgian diaspora in the 1980s. There is something particular about Irish culture that makes it respond in this way to economic recession. And, more and more, it is hard to dismiss the idea that one of these particular things is the sense of internal exile, the sense that Irish people feel less and less at home in Ireland, that Ireland has become somehow unreal. In one way or another, very many Irish people have experienced a sense of the familiar becoming unknown, unrecognisable. Ireland has become so multi-layered, so much a matter of one set of images superimposed on another, that it is hard to tell home from abroad. Thirty-five years of being an offshore economic dependency of the United States have left us with a society that is seen by an increasing number of its young people as a pale imitation of the Real Thing across the Atlantic.

The Americanisation of Ireland that began with the construction of Ireland as a European base for multinational companies has fundamentally altered the meaning of emigration itself. Since Ireland has become in some respects a little America, emigration can no longer be posited as a shift from one state of being to another. A change of location no longer implies a complete change of lifestyle, as it did for, say, a farm labourer from Mayo going to Boston in the 1920s. In significant ways, America has already come to Mayo.

For the generation of Irish writers that grew up after this belated industrial revolution was under way, that process of alteration has also been a process of estrangement. Home has become as unfamiliar as abroad. Because Irish places have themselves been radically changed, it has been possible, in a sense, to emigrate without leaving the island. Everything begins to exist in a state of internal exile. The difference between home and abroad has shrunk to virtually nothing.

Nostalgia for a homeland has lost its meaning, not least because the images of a natural landscape that once constituted memories of home for emigrants from a predominantly rural society have been replaced by memories of a predominantly urban Irish society. What can be remembered, even from exile, is no longer a lost homeland that represents a different state of being, but a place that is of essentially the same kind as the place in which the exile now lives, all the more so because memory itself is now saturated with globalised media images.

A good example is Michael O'Loughlin's poem *The Fugitive*, published in 1982.[10] The opening is conventional, evoking as it does an Irish exile in Paris:

> *In the hour before the Metro opens*
> *I remember you...*

But the next words are not, as might be expected, 'Ireland', or 'mother', but 'Richard Kimble'. Richard Kimble was the eponymous fugitive in the American television series of the 1960s, and the exile's memory is of watching the programme as a child at home in Dublin. An exiled Irish poet's memory of home from Paris is a memory of America:

> *I can't remember the stories now*
> *But in the end it's only the icons that matter,*
> *The silent, anonymous American city*
> *With the rain running down the gutter.*

For a generation that grew up on American television shows, America will always be interwoven with memories of an Irish homeland and an Irish childhood:

> *The muffled snarl of American accents*
> *Coming in loud and razor sharp*
> *Over the local interference.*

This interplay of American accents and local interference is taken to its logical, and comic, conclusion in Roddy Doyle's *The Commitments,* where identity itself, for young working-class Dubliners is a matter of identification with American black music:

'Where are yis from? (He answered the question himself) — Dublin. (He asked another one.) — Wha' part o' Dublin? Barrytown. Wha' class are yis? Workin' class. Are yis proud of it? Yeah, yis are. (Then a practical question) — who buys the most records? The workin' class. Are yis with me? (Not really) — your music should be abou' where you're from an' the sort of people yeh come from. — - — - Say it once, say it loud, I'm black an' I'm proud. They looked at him — James Brown.' [11]

When 'where you're from' is best expressed through the music of blacks in industrial American cities, how can you feel nostalgic for home if you're Irish and living in one of those American cities? And, furthermore, even this way of remembering is no longer distinctively Irish. It is itself an aspect of a global cultural shift, of what Frederic Jameson calls 'the cultural logic of late capitalism'. Jameson remarks that, with the collapse of the high modernist ideology of style, 'the producers of culture have nowhere else to turn but to the past: the imitation of dead styles, speech through all the masks and voices stored up in the imaginary museum of a now global culture.' But the past is itself saturated in electronic imagery: it has itself 'become a vast collection of images, a multitudinous photographic simulacrum'. [12] Culture — in the form of received images of, say, Richard Kimble or James Brown — becomes what nature used to be — a kind of second nature.

And if nostalgia in the old sense is impossible, so is return. The exile's dream of return has no meaning when the homeland is an ex-isle, a place forever gone. Dermot Bolger's poem and play, *The Lament for Arthur Cleary*, [13] hark back to Eibhlin Dubh Ní Chonaill's eighteenth century *Caoineadh Art Ui Laoghaire,* in which a returned exile is killed because he no longer knows how to keep his place in a changed Ireland. Bolger's Arthur Cleary comes back to Dublin from Germany 'consumed with nostalgia/ For an identity irretrievably lost':

> *But that world was dead*
> *Though you could not realise it*
> *A grey smudge of estates*
> *Charted the encroaching horizon ...*

Yet it is not, in contemporary Irish culture, returning exiles alone who sense that the world they knew has gone. One of the most sad but comforting things about emigration used to be the tragi-comic figure of the Returned Yank. Sad because of the sense of loss, the incomprehension at the fact that everything was different from the way it was remembered. Comforting because that incomprehension eased our sense of inferiority, told us that we were the ones who really knew, we were really on top of this place. Now we are all Returned Yanks, looking around us and saying gee, didn't there used to be a pub there, didn't that place look different. didn't I know that guy? And like the Returned Yanks it is easier to go back to a place that is less complicated, less haunted by its own past, to get on the plane and go home to America, regretful but relieved.

In the new, shifting, ill-defined emigration of the 1980s and 1990s, where many young Irish people found themselves in more or less constant motion, in and out of Ireland as the fluctuations of the world economy made them alternately in demand and surplus to requirements, it was no longer possible to pretend that there was a given Irish culture to be lost or held on to. And Irish writers began to reflect much more directly a sense that Ireland was a set of questions and contests rather than a given landscape waiting to be read. The relevant difference is no longer that between home and abroad, but that between the Irish themselves. Exile becomes a prism through which the diverse social forces within Ireland are separated and revealed. The Irish abroad are now written about as people divided from each other by politics, class and sexuality rather than as a single category of humanity divided from a homogenous homeland by exile.

That notion of internal exile, of an Ireland that has become, in a sense, a foreign country for many of its people, whether they stay or go, marks a profound change in the way Irish culture construes emigration. Exile is no longer a process in which a fixed identity is traded for an anonymous and impermanent one.

The only way Irish culture can respond is to replace the map of a place with a map of the journeys of its people. What is important is that such maps will depend on a sense of identity that is entirely imaginative, though not imaginary. The connections they will chart are not physical but cultural, matters not of a past that can be read but of a present and future that have to be constantly written and re-written. And in that writing and re-writing, the Irish abroad will have just as much of a claim on the creation of Irish culture as do the Irish at home.

In the 1990s, America and Ireland represent not opposites, not a dialogue of modernity and tradition, but a continual intertwining in which far from Ireland being the past, and America being the future, America can constitute Ireland's past and Ireland can invent America's future. In the mid-1980s for instance, it was an Irish rock band, U2, which embodied mythic America for the world at large, through their use of the deserts of Colorado and Arizona as a dream landscape in their photographic images, their films *Under a Blood Red Sky* and *Rattle and Hum,* their carefully worked-out Wild West costuming, and their post-apocalyptic born-again lyrics which used the desert as the image of a world after the nuclear holocaust.

Conversely, in the mid-1990s, the international image of traditional Irish culture was constituted most powerfully by *Riverdance,* the Irish dance show that had its origins in the Eurovision Song Contest and that was essentially a product of the Irish diaspora in America, its choreographer and two principal dancers being American-born. When young Irish people can best embody an American dream, and young Americans can best represent Irish tradition to the world, we are dealing not with anything so simple as cultural domination or even so rational as cultural exchange, but with something obsessive, repetitive, continually unfinished, all the time renewing itself in old ways. We are dealing with the ways in which the notion of America itself is an Irish invention, the notion of Ireland an American invention. When we step into this divide, we step into, not an open space, but a hall of mirrors.

Irish writers have coped with this by destroying the old ideology of the indigenous and the alien. Their precursor, as it were, is not the James Joyce of *Ulysses,* obsessively re-creating the detail of Dublin streets from exile, but the Joyce of *Finnegan's Wake,* for whom Dublin is but a template of all other places, linked linguistically to any other point on the globe. Just as, for the later Joyce, Dublin is also Lublin, West Munster is also Westminster and Crumlin is the Kremlin, the Ireland of the 1990s is, for its writers, also America and Europe. It is a linguistic, imaginative Ireland, an Ireland that cannot be read but must always be written. The writer who first found this way of encompassing Irish reality is the poet Paul Durcan. He found it partly through what might otherwise be regarded as realistic description of a visible and recognisable Ireland:

> *We live in a Georgian, Tudor, Classical Greek,*
> *Moorish, Spanish Hacienda, Regency Period*
> *Ranch-house, Three-Storey Bungalow*
> *On the edge of the edge of town:*
> *'Poor Joe's Row' —*
> *The townspeople call it -*
> *But our real address is 'Ronald Reagan Hill',*
> *- That vulturous-looking man in the States.* [14]

The movement of these lines, through a random succession of periods and places, through a landscape where even the names of places are unstable, where a woman starts to describe her home in Tipperary and ends up in the United States, is emblematic of contemporary Irish culture. Place in Paul Durcan's poems is unstable, permeable, unbounded. Durcan's Ireland exists, not just in familiar place-names, but in such surreal yet meaningful places as 'the east European parts of Dublin city', 'the road from Mayo into Egypt', 'Westport in the Light of Asia Minor', 'Africa on the West Coast of Kerry', 'the Kalahari, Pimlico, and the West of Ireland', 'The Dublin-Paris-Berlin-Moscow Line', 'a French Ireland'.

These places belong on maps that can be measured not with the metres that derive from a fixed, immutable length of metal in Paris, but from the passage of light through time. Ireland has started to imagine itself in the way that photographers imagine the world, measuring distance by the motion of light rather than by a fixed, unmoving object. Its imagined metres and centimetres are the marks of human journeys across the landscape. And it is driven by a desire as old as humanity itself but one that is especially strong in the 1990s world where global connections have made the world no less inscrutable and no more homely. It is the desire for safe passage, the desire for an endless ball of thread with which to mark our way in the labyrinth, so that we can always retrace our steps, the desire for true lines through a map of the world.

In November 1995, the Minor Planet Centre in Cambridge, Massachusetts decided to name Minor Planet 5029, an asteroid recently discovered somewhere between Mars and Jupiter, 'Ireland'. Minor Planet Ireland is far away and virtually invisible to the naked eye and almost nothing is known about its composition. It bears, in other words, a similar relationship to the terrestrial Ireland as the emergent Ireland of imaginative connections does to the physical Ireland in the Atlantic. Spinning in the dark, held in place by the pull of invisible gravity, it is still solid, full of possibilities, and, perhaps, inhabitable.

FOOTNOTES

1. Henry Louis Gates Jnr. *Colored People: A Memoir*, London, Viking, 1995, p.5.
2. Padraic O Conaire, *Exile*, trans. by Gearailt MacEoin, Clo Iar-Chonnachta, 1994. p.104.
3. Walter Benjamin, *The Storyteller*, in Illuminations, Fontana, London, 1973. p.84 — 85.
4. *The Short Stories of Liam O"Flaherty*, New English Library, London, 1966. p.103.
5. ibid. p.260.
6. David Fitzpatrick, *Oceans of Consolation: Personal Accounts of Irish Migration to Australia*, Cork University Press, 1994, p.620.
7. Fitzpatrick, p.624.
8. ibid, p.627.
9. Sebastian Barry, *Prayers of Sherkin and Boss Grady's Boys*, Methuen, London, 1991, p.13.
10. In *Atlantic Blues*, Raven Arts Press, Dublin, 1982, p.28-29.
11. Roddy Doyle, *The Commitments*, King Farouk, Dublin, 1987, p.7 — 8.
12. Frederic Jameson, *Postmodernism or the Cultural Logic of Late Capitalism*, Verso, London and New York, 1991, p.17-18.
13. The poem is in *Internal Exiles*, Dolmen Press, Portlaoise, 1987, p.67 ff.
14. *The Haulier's Wife Meets Jesus on the Road Near Moone in The Berlin Wall Cafe*, The Blackstaff Press, Belfast, 1985.p.4.

Everything is Political in a Divided Society

John Hume MEP

'Our island is full of comfortless noises' wrote Seamus Heaney in his 1979 collection, *Field Work*. His refusal to yield to this traditional and dangerous pattern explains why today he holds the Nobel Prize for Literature. Like his counterparts in literature and the other arts, he has always been a voice for reason and imagination standing out against the noise of unreason and hatred.

The cultural riches of Ireland provide a stark contrast with the sterility of the political conflict which has divided our island for so long. It is very much to the credit of our artists and writers that they resisted the temptation to deepen the political conflict. They avoided being drawn into service in political quarrels and refused to contribute either to the expression or the intensification of the centuries-old divisions of the people of this island. Far from upholding and solidifying cultural divisions, which would have been the easy option, they attempted to analyse them and to demonstrate the decadence of old ideologies.

Given the historic connections between violence and culture in Ireland, from the remote origins to very recently, this is a very substantial victory over deep but outmoded passions. We should honour those who opened up this new path. In the past, many of the most celebrated creators of all traditions did not see violence as a problem. Indeed,

Everything is Political in a Divided Society

some of them were often up to their necks in violence, (some even paying with their necks too). The generation which has lived through all or part of the Troubles is the first in which poets refused to eulogise violence and in which writers and artists in general did not genuflect before the traditional prejudices of their fellow citizens. It is important to note that this new reality applies, irrespective of their diverse origins and traditions.

As a result, we have had more literature than propaganda over the last twenty-five years. Even in the works most connected with politics, propaganda is noticeable by its absence. For example, Brian Friel's *The Freedom of the City*, despite its committed analysis of the Northern situation, is clearly not a piece of agit-prop.

In rejecting the role of tribal tribunes, merely articulating the views of our divided society, poets, novelists, playwrights and others served our society very well. The vision of an alternative society, where difference is respected and celebrated rather than condemned or exorcised, has been established. Respect for diversity and difference being at the heart of the conflict, they pointed towards its ultimate resolution. No present-day writer is obliged to face up personally to W.B.Yeats' anguished reflection over whether his words had sent men to their deaths. Fortunately, contemporary writers and artists demonstrated beyond doubt their commitment to life rather than the traditional obsession with death.

This is all the more praiseworthy in a divided society such as ours where everything is politicised. Our society is criss-crossed by cultural, historical, religious, political and economic divisions that have given rise to centuries of violence, political instability and economic underdevelopment. Twenty-five years of violence from 1969 accentuated these divisions and politicised all aspects of life, and indeed of death. The moral and intellectual strength needed to resist the siren calls of traditional ideologies and the weight of personal loyalties to one section or another of the community should not be underestimated. Working to dispel false certainties has been difficult but essential. As a general rule, fanaticism and the claim to have a monopoly on truth vary inversely with the ability and the will to attempt to grasp the complexities of our society, and proportionately with the fear of difference.

By avoiding the temptation to cling to the traditional blocs, writers and artists helped to make our divisions less acute. They opened the path for the examination and analysis of our complex society, of the differences between traditions and the common aspects linking them. Such work is therefore profoundly political without being partisan. Advocating openness, they are the enemies of the 'dread closure' to use Tom Paulin's phrase. In so doing they helped to provide cultural signposts towards the political resolution of our ancient quarrel.

Contemporary cultural life in Ireland distinguishes itself from the past through its non-partisan involvement in the reality of Irish society. We have suffered too much from the over-intimate relationship between politics and culture in the past. At last, a middle way between 'art for art's sake' and the total politicisation of culture has been found. Today, it is clear that cultural activity is inseparable from social realities but it is no longer a simple reflection of those realities. Perhaps for the first time, we now recognise the autonomy of culture as a value in its own right. As a result, the diversity of identities on this island is reflected in cultural life.

This diversity is becoming increasingly apparent. Just to cite one example, the range of literature extends from the suburban novels of Roddy Doyle to the pastoral poetry of Seamus Heaney. However, a common thread links very diverse writers and artists, their connection with both the real and the imagination in contemporary Ireland. We are finally benefitting from a cultural life which reveals, and is deeply rooted in, the diversity of Irish society but which rejects all forms of exclusivity and intolerance. The Single Irish Thought no longer exists. At the same time, we have avoided the retreat into 'volkisch' culture but without abandoning the diverse identities which characterise the island.

Seamus Heaney found the right note when he wrote: 'the object of art is peace'. This is not a political slogan but a moral imperative. It is a question above all of demonstrating the possibilities of alternative, and thus peaceful, modes of existence. To cite Seamus Heaney once again: 'You have to change what's there. You have to transform it'. In this sense, he can be considered the representative figure of Irish cultural life.

Seamus Heaney's definition changes the nature of artistic endeavour in Ireland. Every culture serves in part to celebrate or defend a particular way of life. But if it confines itself to those limits, the risk of sclerosis is great. In a divided society, the 'defence and illustration' style of culture is very dangerous. Fortunately, our writers and artists faced up to the challenge of establishing critical modes of enquiry. In so doing, they have fulfilled their prime obligation — forcing everyone to think, to think differently and to search for new forms of political and social organisation. If we are to resolve our conflict, everyone has to abandon failed ideologies and invent new perspectives. Clearly, we have made more cultural than political progress, but we can and should build upon this to achieve a political settlement. Whether we do so or not depends on the extent to which governments and political parties face up to their obligations to think and to demonstrate some imagination.

The slogan 'power to the imagination' derives from the events of 1968 in France. An Irish equivalent is needed. Whilst writers and artists seized upon the power of the imagination, imagination must now be employed in politics. A vision of a different future in which the right to difference will be guaranteed is needed. We must envisage political structures which command the allegiance of all citizens and in which power is exercised fairly. Above all, the imaginary and illusionary past which lead us to the violence of the last decades must be rejected. We must avoid the traps which would condemn us to watching, in the words of Thomas Kinsella, 'two more cardboard kings join/in one more battle of the Boyne.'

Writers and artists also played a very important role in opening up Ireland to the outside world. Before the 1960s, the country stagnated in isolationism. Though one can understand the good intentions of its architects, the autarchic utopia of economic and cultural isolation resulted in the slow haemorrhage of Irish society. Since then, Ireland has become a very open country which is firmly behind European integration. The importance of culture in this evolution cannot be underestimated. Today it is beyond doubt that contemporary Irish culture is an integral part of Europe's cultural heritage and future.

The cultural balance of payments between Ireland and Europe is now in equilibrium. We import as well as export. Ireland is very open to developments in the wider world. It is interesting to note that many of our writers have translated the work of other European authors, both from the West and the East. Similarly, writers in Irish are no longer confined to the task of preserving the 'hidden Ireland' but play their part in European networks dedicated to the translation of Irish-language texts into other European languages as well as the translation into Irish of texts in other European languages. Literature in Irish is no longer an under-privileged relation of literature in English. Indeed, Dublin can also be described as the capital of linguistic diversity in Europe since it is the seat of the European Bureau for Lesser Used Languages. The recognition that all languages are important is significant for all European languages as one is always in a minority somewhere.

Everything is Political in a Divided Society

Having lived through a cultural renaissance, the political resolution of our divisions is overdue. If we succeed in creating new and agreed political structures, we will have repaid our debt to the creative forces of this country.

What lesson can be learned from the cultural renewal of our country? The answer is simple. The existence of cultural diversity must be reflected in our political institutions. The right to difference must be respected.

The chance of establishing a permanent peace in Ireland exists. It is necessary to complete the political modernisation which alone will permit us to face the challenges of the rapidly-approaching new century. The absence of violence would offer us the chance, for the first time in our history, to address real economic and social problems, to establish a new democracy and to play our part at the heart of modern Europe.

There are two great challenges to face. First, how to make the most out of the diversity of our society? Second, how to adapt to globalisation?

Diversity is a real asset for both Ireland and Europe. Differences of nationality, culture and race are part of human nature. No two individuals in the world are identical. We should accept these fundamental realities and turn them to our advantage. Difference and diversity too often are considered as threats. Ireland has suffered much from the practical consequences of such a mindset. Over 3,000 people have died because of the failure to respect the right to diversity. Intolerance of difference is the pathway to death and destruction.

Faced with difference, there are three possibilities. One can attempt to pretend that it does not exist, a strategy that has ultimately failed wherever it has been employed. The second possibility, the eradication of difference, has marked our century with the dishonourable seals of war and massacres. Violence is not an effective way of dealing with difference. Violence breeds violence, leading to the vicious spiral of an eye for an eye. But the policy of an eye for an eye only succeeds in leaving everyone blind.

Since we cannot pretend that difference does not exist and it cannot be eradicated without committing terrible crimes, we must exploit it for our benefit. We have to look for agreement, for institutions and ways of life that permit the diverse sections of our society to live together while preserving those identities and differences.

Europe enjoys an incredible richness of cultural diversity. Our indigenous cultures and traditions have been reinforced by the contribution of the cultures of every continent on the planet. We have to work together to defend difference. To defend the culture of others is to protect one's own culture.

Globalisation of society also demands new responses. This is the first generation of humanity for whom the world has become one. We are the first to inhabit a planet where the world is part of our consciousness and of our daily life. Most of our ancestors lived in a much more confined universe in which the framework of awareness was the village, the town, the region and perhaps the country. Day by day, we are discovering that the future of the human race will be determined collectively, not by individual states or nations.

Daily life can be changed by events on the other side of the planet. Increasingly internationalised communications permit rapid contacts between the countries of the world. Nationally-based virtual monopolies of information and communication markets are no longer viable. Mass media and their owners no longer have a nationality, nor are they part of a specific political system. Just like Hollywood in terms of popular culture, Atlanta is laying its claim to be the world capital of news.

Cultural and economic globalisation calls into question established rights and practices. Traditional frameworks are breaking down while tried and tested political systems no longer function as they did in the past. It is not surprising therefore that traditional ideas on the organisation of political power at the national level, which have dominated western society for more than two hundred years, should be questioned.

The great political enterprise of the future will be the construction and maintenance of open and inclusive societies. Exclusiveness and defeatism must be resisted. Political systems must be adapted to the diversity and complexity of our societies. Each society must be organised to allow it to take part effectively and fairly in globalisation. Combatting social exclusion and establishing the rights of all to be citizens on an equal basis must be at the centre of the preoccupations of political systems.

The renewal of Ireland is scarcely thinkable outside the process of the development of a political and cultural Europe. The importance of the European Union and its innovative institutions is undeniable. The European Union is above all a force for peace. It is the greatest example of conflict resolution in the history of humanity. Nations who for centuries invaded each other, occupied each other's territories, expelled each other's peoples and massacred each other, came together freely to bury their old hatreds. They united to pursue their common interests and to rule out war as a means of settling their differences. This is a remarkable achievement in its own right. But the fact that these nations have preserved their identities is even more encouraging. It proves that institutions can be created to pursue common objectives without sacrificing Europe's diversity of culture and traditions. It proves extraordinarily clearly that diversity is neither a weakness nor a threat. We have already demonstrated the capacity to reconcile joint action and difference. Efforts must be re-doubled and institutions adapted to ensure that an enlarged European Union will continue on the same track.

Political entities always work better when the importance of diversity is taken into account. Regional variations are, in this respect, very significant. It does not appear to be an accident that the majority of the richest regions in Europe benefit from strong regional institutions. By liberating individuals and communities, by reducing the social and geographical gap between the citizen and the state and by facilitating a diversity of flexible responses, energies are channelled towards the search for innovation, effectiveness, employment and prosperity. Decentralisation encourages constructive involvement in the decision-making process and in development strategies. The more people are given responsibility for their future, the more they show their ability to take such responsibility. The more people believe that their political institutions belong to them, the more effective those institutions will be. Decentralisation is, in a sense, the prime weapon in the fight against social exclusion and for the renovation of democracy.

Working for a new Ireland in a new Europe, we can gain much from the lessons learnt in the cultural life of this island. We should take some inspiration from the example of our writers and artists. All the political organisations on our island must elaborate a vision of a new Ireland. It is time to look honestly at the virtues and defects of our society and find new answers capable of preparing us for the challenges which lie ahead. It is time to paint a realistic portrait of society and to abandon the consolation of outmoded imaginary mental pictures. We need the courage to imagine new perspectives which will help us to formulate answers to the questions of social diversity, possible political institutions and the eventual resolution of our conflict. Above all, we need the imagination to look to the future and to the outside world and to transform our island into a symbol of hope.

Irish Art, An Art of Journeying and Dislocations

Liam Kelly

Place, in Jack B. Yeats' late paintings, is as indeterminate as his use of time. It harbours a national longing but resists settlement. Everything is on the move; the paint, the people, the light. The numen of this place is always nomadic, restless and rootless. Yeats' world induces states of wandering. Brian O'Doherty has written that Irish lives are lived out between promise and regret — the future full of regret and the past full of promise.

'Promise and regret can be equated with two phases — "before it starts" and "when it's over". Almost all Yeats' paintings belong to these two formidable armies. On the one hand — youth, dawn, horses, encounters, gambling etcetera, on the other — darkness, departures, evening, age, singing, commemorations, story-telling reading. Common to both is the idea of "travelling".' [1]

If the land (bogland), in the earlier poetry of Seamus Heaney, is the great repository, a national memory bank, light is the great revealer in the painting of Jack Yeats. With Heaney the act of poetry is an act of excavation, with Yeats it is an act of investment in pigment and colour. Both acts are connected with a search and certainly in Yeats' painting with freedom. And in turn, freedom with Yeats is expressed by way of a travelling mode — a coming and a going. Heaney talks of *'poetry as a point of entry into the buried life of the feelings or as a point of exit for it.'* [2]

Yeats is as relevant today as ever before, and, as we will see, the concept of itinerary has proved useful for many young Irish artists, among them Diarmuid Delargy and Kathy Prendergast, as a way of exploring landscape for socio-political meanings and concerns, as well as more personal feelings.

Kathy Prendergast, a southern Irish artist, has been drawn to Heaney's poetry. Chalk is a material that the artist has been attracted to in recent years. She has used it as a dry stone wall in *Another Country,* (exhibited at Rosc, Dublin, 1988). More recently it became a raised chalk bed, like a cairn, with a simple white or, perhaps more accurately, cream mattress placed along the length of it on top. The title of the work *A Dream of Discipline* (1989) comes from a Seamus Heaney poem where he refers to someone's bed as 'a dream of discipline'. Prendergast here lays out the mattress to find its new topography as it settles on the stones. There is a reversal of sleeping here: a new presence and absence. The cairn traditionally marked a grave, the chalk makes it expressionless and the mattress becomes a cushion against time.

Kathy Prendergast is conscious of being reared on an island, always looking out. Ireland and emigration clearly underwrite some of the notions at work, as does the concept of a contained culture. Her work is about quietude and isolation. It minimises activity while journeying; it materialises interludes along the way. The work conjures with dualities: male/female; hard/soft; body/land; macro/micro; silences/containments. She is on a cosmic archeological dig that pursues time and leaves us markings as to where she might be.

By contrast, Diarmuid Delargy subverts any quietudes and classical repose to set up wanderings in a lost Eden. He unsteadies everything. Animals hover on the verge of a reckless stampede. Nomadic figures, in groupings, seek after something never to attain it. There are dislocations at work. It is as if the land goes into a time shift for an examination of the human condition taken out of immediate historical events and happenings. Delargy calls up a Mediterranean, figurative, Utopia but played out in a Northern temperate climate. Trees hold, within their forms, forebodings. There is the feeling that the natural elements know, but cannot reveal even under intensive questioning. The only recourse is to move on; to search further.

In *On Through the Not so Quiet Lands,* (1983) Delargy plays off Jack B Yeats' *On Through the Silent Lands,* (1951). Power lines are down, communication interfered with. A black flag leans, disconsolate. A spectral figure follows his donkey along a shoreline under an aggressively rendered sky. As in much of the artist's work the earth and the sky play equally proportionate roles.

As a printmaker, Delargy has few equals in Ireland, in an art form that has often carried sweet images of pastoral retreat. The marks of his drawing technique never find fixed, formal, definitions but are always in a swirling search for an illusive presence that leave traces of where it has been. There is the corresponding notion that enduring qualities between figures and the land are laid into the land like traces not easily revealed.

An interest in animals extends from childhood rural experiences in rural County Antrim. Aidan Dunne sees a harmony between the land and animals in Delargy's work.

'In his work, animals can be seen as exemplars of human ideas, emotions and activities and they can be seen as indicating an harmonious relationship with the landscape.' [3]

This may be true of his use of the horse as a symbol of freedom and the Utopian ideal. However it is not so true of the pig as the animal of the factual 'now'. Compare his painting of *Sleeping Venus,* (1989) with his earlier etching *Sleeping Venus,* (1987). In the former painting we witness

Venus as serene beauty who fits comfortably the contours of the land. In the etching we have the pig exposed on the land as crude victim. It will be further dismembered in *Crubeens I,* (1989). Here we have a contrast between the artistic affinity with the world of Giorgione (the world of Art and idealism) and the world of social reality coming through experience of a particular place, a particular time viz. the turbulence of political upheaval in the North of Ireland.

In more recent work Delargy's figure groupings increase in number, becoming less confined in space; larger vistas, panoramas open up. The dangers of inbreeding (the tribal North) and narcissism (preoccupation with identity) loom large in *'The Trees were Witness'*, (1988). Again Aidan Dunne observes.

'A feeling of flouted harmony, of something being amiss, is unmistakable. The arcadian idyll is certainly threatened'. [4]

The references to the political problems in Ulster are always oblique and filtered through a dislocated illusory space, and like the late paintings of J.B. Yeats they are doubly encoded: universal in scope but extending out of an Irish experience. This is the importance of the reverberations in Delargy's vision; the correspondences among the trees in his paintings and prints.

Marie Barrett's psychological studies of cultural dislocations, heightened states of confusion and alienation are worked up from meanings in the experience of returning to live in a small borderland town, Buncrana, Co. Donegal. The town like other parts of Donegal forms part of the natural and spiritual hinterland of Derry, just a few miles away in Northern Ireland.

The social pressures and cultural clashes of living in a small conservative community are thrown into vivid contrast by the knowledge both direct and indirect of a wider world. In her drawings of machines of war, submarines, helicopters, jet fighters serve as absurd dislocations to disturb the apparent rural calm. But this intrusion of the hardware of war is only a sign of what is wrong: the cause is long-standing and more complicated. Her naked psychologically emaciated figures contribute to this 'landscape as asylum' approach by the vulnerability of their upright gait and fixed facial staring. Barrett's drawing technique also contributes. By scoring and hacking she builds up a blackness on the surface that robs the landscape of any suggestion of stability. Comparisons can be made with Dermot Seymour's absurd juxtapositions of animals and machines and also the hallucinatory drawings of Cork artist Julie Kellegher. The artists, however, who naturally come to mind as influences and whom the artist acknowledges are Rembrandt and Goya. Both artists knew how to set up contrasts of light and darkness to graphically fix and probe states of psychological unease. Likewise Barrett can effectively record concealments and revelations, extending the emotional impact by the use of text in an unsteady calligraphy.

The artist believes that in the past the Catholic church in Ireland has placed more emphasis on death than life and that this is particularly felt in a rural community. It is the 'vale of tears' syndrome. [5] You are just passing through this life, you have a cross to bear. Consequently there is less facing up to issues. It would seem that Barrett reflects this attitude in *Politics of Aspiration and Commemoration,* (1987). The body here is of temporary occupation and health care is perhaps more spiritual than physical. In the drawing, flowers, both drawn and applied (pressed flowers), carry the symbolism of commemoration, a calf juts its head around the tombstone and the flanking figure seems anguished but resigned. In Donegal, rural isolation without social contact has led to a high rate of depression among women — another contradiction in the romantic, soothing, therapeutic image of the land. Barrett's females are withdrawn and skeletal, without much control over their own bodies or minds — tranquillised and managed by others. In *Madonna with Helicopters*, (1989) the artist calls forth the evidence while in *Factory Girl Donegal*, (1991) our sister now working for a multi-national textile firm, is offered financial incentives to keep America solvent and production continuous.

Barrett is interested as much in the problems men face in society, as in women's problems. In a series of drawings such as *Faith of our Fathers*, (1988) she pins medals on sagging naked flesh to painfully stress the blind and contradictory acceptance of the ritualistic power of the emblems of war. Whether it is a Celtic torque necklace or a decoration for fighting at the Somme during the First World War, Barrett condemns the tribal glorification of death and martyrdom. The experience of having a relative fight and die at the Somme — a Donegal Catholic at that — whose medal of honour and glory is still in the family offered another set of confusions and allusions to work out.

Marie Barrett is concerned about the push and pull of emigration, not only in her drawings, but also in her public art piece *Target Figures*, (1989), in which she moored suitcases in the River Foyle. Like education, emigration has a distancing effect. But the artist can see the humorous as well as the serious side to its effects. In *Ex Pat Inis Eoghain 100*, (1991) a disorientated and bewildered male stands in one garden of delights away from an apparently other garden of delights. Whether it is the anticipated dream or the shock of a return, what is clear is that an irretrievable transformation has occurred. It is similar to the effect of education on someone from a working class environment. His or her place within the former family and community network of relations is never quite the same. The artist herself, by virtue of the information she carries around, and her art practice, will always be somewhat distanced no matter how affable she may appear. This is beautifully mocked at in the drawing *How the Man from Clones Grappled with the Ideas in the*

Tauromaquia, (1987). Goya it may be said has not had the same effect on everybody.

Ronnie Hughes, like Marie Barrett, spent a year in New York and is concerned to demythologise cultural perceptions of Irishness as projected abroad, particularly in America, and their attendant fallout for the emigrant as well as the effects of their re-bounding in Ireland. One effect, as Hughes sees it, of the Tourist Board projection of Ireland as a rural unspoilt rugged landscape of honest toil, is that the emigrant, however well educated. is viewed as an unskilled peasant fit for unsophisticated work. The other concern of the artist is the unthinking contribution by Americans of money to Ireland which, he would claim, may be misused for violent activities.

Hughes' artistic technique is to juxtapose or intermingle images: those representing a culturally loaded past with the reality of the present. The result is to set up a situational irony. The notion of emigration as a herding instinct is worked through in two paintings. In *The Final Cut*, (1991) passengers queue for a flight at Shannon Airport, facilitated by U.S. Immigration Offices available before embarkation, rather than the usual procedure after arrival. Superimposed on this central image is a semi abstract herd of sheep, increased in scale, with a serial pattern of yellow baggage labels intermingled with them. The optical construction of the sheep herd only reveals itself slowly, to carry the intended irony at work. Similarly in *Rural Insulation*, (1991) the closeness of society in Ireland is revealed to also have a suffocating effect. A more realistic painting of sheep here encloses a central group of four Irish people.

Many Irish emigrants have found work in the building industry in America and Hughes is fond of the linguistic interplay of his deconstructive technique on the construction industry. In *Ghost Workers (Great Irish Erections)*, (1991) the repeated image of a construction worker sitting on the steel framework of a building is set amongst Irish historical building relics of the past. The work allows for a variety of readings, among them the contradiction of the Irish worker contributing now to corporate America as a manual worker amidst the cultural achievement of his own past — inheritance as a positive and negative construction of identity. The same theme is perhaps more poetically endowed in *Constructed Heritage*, (1991) where the dim pattern of a building worker in green outline with yellow hard hat is spread across a spade marked section of brown bog, like a cultivated bog flower for export.

As well as expressing these concerns in painting Hughes has also made an installation titled *Consummation* at the Orpheus Gallery 1992 and a time based work, *Correspondence,* (1993) at the Crescent Arts Centre, both in Belfast. *Correspondence* was part of a Denver/Belfast exchange project. The American artist, Mark Lunning, with whom Hughes was twinned, proposed an exchange of objects by mail which were relevant to their respective locations. Hughes sent fragments of stone from bombed out Belfast buildings of which he has a collection. On the stones which he received he painted images of new buildings in Belfast. These were then thrown through a window of the Crescent Centre to form a shattered installation of their intent on the floor of the gallery interior. The pieces of broken glass were each bandaged where they had fallen. The work was intended to parallel the results of American intervention in Northern Ireland with its attendant damage and repair.

The Orpheus installation, *Consummation,* was more lighthearted in intention and presentation. A large 'chair' was composed of some 106 green plastic beer crates, each crate holding their empty bottles. It faced the gallery wall which had 32 Harp and Guinness beer bottles placed on individual shelves with their labels over painted by hand, illustrating typical images of Ireland as expressed in typical tourist brochures. The work compares with John

Irish Art, An Art of Journeying and Dislocations

Carson's *A bottle of Stout in every pub in Buncrana* but here by way of inflated presentation of the stereotyping bringing together the Irish Emigrant's capacity for sentimentality, in direct proportion to his capacity for drink.

Emigration, however, is a complex phenomenon and requires more penetrative probing than youthful hacking. The Irish visual arts has only begun to reveal the layers of the complexities and forces at work in this aspect of transculturation.

Cathy Harper's work takes us into dangerous territories: the bog and art in cathartic mode. Seamus Heaney has used the bog so effectively as a political metaphor, and purgation in art can so readily lead to theatricality that avoidance is perhaps the prudent path. But for Harper, who originally studied constructed textiles, the fibrous earth seemed the appropriate vehicle for the exploration of trapped nerves.

The life/death/rebirth cycle of the bog is a generating force that allows for resurrection and transfiguration. And during this natural process, the earth conceals, retains, preserves but transforms when it offers up. Harper, like Heaney, was fascinated by the Danish bodies in Tollund.[6] These bodies are remarkable in their form and details but the peat has 'cured' them into grotesque exhibits: they embody in their grimace a sacrificial hurt like a baby's entry cry into this world.

It is within this condition that Harper explores her own emotional responses to birth and parenthood. Harper sees conception as a terrible gamble:

'The ignition of life deep within the womb begins a journey. That "immaculate conception" "preserved immaculate from all stain" is held, as the bog people are held within the bog, in a state of suspension. Conflict, rage, confrontation within the real world have no bearing on that state of unreality. Ejection from the womb, or a tearing of a

115

body from the bog, is the beginning then. The unreality is rudely shattered and the "staining" begins.' [7]

This view, however, does not allow for nature, only culture. The staining has already begun in the inherited genes. The neo-nate or a bog has a history.

Catherine Harper uses natural bog materials together with paint, glue and fibre in *Conceptua Immaculata,* (1991). Fleece, rope and sheep dung are constructed into an installation piece which creates metaphorically a wolf in sheep's clothing. It is a message to man as wayward patriarch with a gold nugget phallic symbol placed appropriately. Guilt, family abandonment and betrayal are being faced up to rather than expurgated.

Ourselves Alone, (1991) celebrates her mother within a family of three as protector and provider — indeed as sacrificial victim. But woman can also be wayward and predatory as suggested by *That Treacherous Lecherous One,* (1991) — woman as sexual manipulator can also betray. A fibrous Sheelagh-na-gig with inflated, all consuming vagina — becomes a fatal attraction. It recalls Heaney's lines, from *The Tollund Man,*

> *'She tightened her torc on him*
> *And opened her fen*
> *Those dark juices working*
> *Him to a saint's kept body.'* [8]

The danger here is that like the exposed internal organs in some of the artist's works, guilt ties everyone up and the unravelling becomes more and more complex and like the living bog continues to be cyclic.

Dermot Seymour's lurid, ominous and displaced Drumlin borderlands are also myth-laden and words are used to explore conundrums, complexities and bizarre juxta- positions. Nothing seems to be what it is. If the Ulster problem is about territory then it is about insecurities. Seymour brands and marks his absurd menagerie of sheep, cattle and pookas so that they only stray into his pictures, just as partisans mark and territorialize the Ulster countryside.

His animals are always the ones who look on, silent witnesses to the persistent fact that nothing has changed or they pick up diseases from the land underlining a preoccupation of the artist — the idea of the sickness in the land. An example of the latter in *Botulism over Mullaghcreevy* (1985), an intriguingly ambiguous painting in which it is difficult to tell if a reclining figure is resting or dead. In the mid-1980's there was a drought in Ireland and seagulls which had contracted the disease botulism from eating off contaminated rubbish tips would fall out of the skies. Seymour has incorporated such an image as a metaphor for the persistence of death associated with his notion of the 'wounded land'. He has commented,

'... the figure is lying there in the sense — is he dead? is he asleep? is he sick?... that's the question mark. Those are just ambiguous conundrums thrown in to start this whole idea that nothing is ever what it seems which for me is one of the ways of trying to come to terms with the complexities of place ... so you start digging.'[9]

Seymour is fond of incorporating military insignia, flags and graffiti as other forms of marking and categorising but it is the titles of his paintings that set the riddles off. His titles, however, do more than describe. They humorously extend the meanings by interlacing them, as in *The Queen's Own Scottish Borderers Observe the King of the Jews peering behind Sean McGuigan's Sheep on the fourth Sunday after Epiphany,* (1988). The words roll together the series of juxtapositions in the imagery: military intrusion and surveillance; religious expression and rural circumstance.

Seymour is also fond of the double take. Here again the titles assist as in *A Friesian Coughed Over Drumshat on the Death of the Reverend George Walker of Kilmore,* (1988). The double take or reference may link an historical figure with a contemporary parallel. Here an inflammatory preacher (an historical legacy) is off-set by a bellowing cow which is suffering from brucellosis, indicated by the inflated shape of her neck, causing her to cough. In other circumstances some of these cows eat fertiliser bags which cause their stomachs to explode. The double take is then extended since the IRA use fertilisers for their explosives.

Seymour has used the Ulster drumlin landscape to enhance his desired sense of vertigo and inherent instability. He has also isolated animals on offshore stacks of land. This is particularly evident in *On the Balcony of the Nation,* (1988), a painting which summarised his concerns up to that time, focusing on a dislocated world of imminent collapse and moral breakdown. Since moving to live in the West of Ireland, Seymour has continued to develop this imagery of disintegration but now under even more dominating and luridly colourful skies.

But the lingering legacy of the North's political troubles still continues to intrude. On first moving to Co. Mayo he completed a 'peripheral' painting, *Summer grazing on Innisclug Under the Weight of the Western Sky in the Last Decade of the Twentieth Century,* (1992). A floating fertiliser bag is now seen above a forlorn cow on a stack against an ominous sky, with Ireland written on it in Japanese, bound for export. It would seem that many other cows are also in danger.

In Ireland surveillance is a kind of national voyeurism where no-one is sure who is the watched or the watcher. It is an infinite regression of an image within an image, within an image, like the structure of a Flann O'Brien novel or the open circular mode of traditional Irish music.

As can be seen there is now more open examination of Irish cultural tradition. And within this tendency text has become important either as carefully considered titles or words superimposed on images or words and slogans worked up from the landscape or townscape itself. Michael Farrell is historically important here.

Towards the end of the sixties and early seventies Farrell's work began to change — the political troubles in Northern Ireland had already begun and Farrell's work which, to date, had no political connotations began to respond to the tragic situation in Ulster.

A series of abstract works, his *Pressè* series, which were purely formal studies, now began to take on meanings that put the formal elements of his visual vocabulary to the service of more politically significant and impelling content. The squelches of 'pop' juice now became blood — the once sterile language of the *Pressè* series became the passionate *Pressè Politique* - anonymity gave way to personal identity.

Variations on this theme continued to become more and more reflective on what it means to be Irish and an artist, rather than merely an artist. In *Une nature morte a la mode Irlandaise,* (1975) we witness newspaper headlines of various tragedies chopped up by the now fulminating *Pressè* elements and the use of witty and clever punning in the deadly appropriate French title on the concept of "nature morte".

In an interview in the *Irish Times* 1977 Farrell reflected upon his artistic change:

'... I became interested more in the literary aspects and less in the formal. It put me in a terrible jam, and rethinking the whole basis of my work took a long time. I've withdrawn from the international stream of art to a more human and personal style then before. I found in my big abstract works that I couldn't say things that I felt like saying. I had arrived at a totally aesthetic art with no literary connotations. I wanted to make statements using sarcasm, or puns, or wit and all of these I could not do before because of the limited means of expression I had adopted.' [10]

Farrell was, by now, living in Paris and from what his new domicile had to offer he chose to deploy Boucher's painting of *Miss O'Murphy* (herself an Irish emigrant living in France and one time mistress of Louis XV) as a more potent symbol for the direction in which his artistic and personal concerns were leading. In one of this series the artist lays out Miss O'Murphy like a piece of meat in a butcher's window signifying the various butcher's cuts 'gigot, forequarters, leg cut, knee cap'. Here, by word play, he both puns upon the name of the original artist, Boucher, and poignantly comments upon the savagery of the political system and its victims in the North of Ireland (knee-capping is a customary punishment carried out by the I.R.A. for informers and the like.) The artist himself has said of these paintings: 'They make every possible statement on the Irish situation, religious, cultural, political, the cruelty, the horror, every aspect of it.' [11] One should add to his list the exploitation of women.

Victor Sloan has produced an impressive body of photoworks which act as a critique of the annual 12th July Orange marches which take place at various venues around the province. Marching here is a form of staking territorial claims with the sound of drums and pipes beating in and rendering that claim; parading an ideology. And Sloan's technique of scraping into the negative, and selectively and subtly overpainting the print, parallels the inherent tensions and the demonstrative and resounding nature of that claim.

The scraping, dancing static of line that the artist uses draws history into every image, allowing it to reverberate, call out and echo. Like Yeats' liquid use of paint Sloan's line journeys up from the past to the present, babbling out in a manic incoherent frenzy. Commenting, on *Walk 8* from the series *The Walk, The Platform and the Field,* (1986) Brian McAvera distinguishes Sloan's technique and strategy from news media photographic records of everyday events.

'His framing of the picture emphasises the foursquare solidity and determination of the marchers : part of a never-ending triumph of the will ... while his scraping of

the pin on the original negative — a series of violent diagonal slashes echoing the ceremonial sword — provides an externalisation of the violence that lies dormant behind the festive surface'. [12]

The title of the series *The Walk, the Platform and the Field,* (1986) encapsulates the political space that Sloan is interrogating. The walk is symbolic of freedom and protest (Protestantism); The 'platform' becomes the base of broadcast for political rhetoric (echoing all the way to Rome) and 'the field' is the emotional ground. Sloan's next series *Drumming,* (1986) continued with the same interests and met with both critical and popular acclaim. As the series title now suggested Sloan 'drummed' this annual occurrence beyond myth: the gestural marks now froze the still photograph into a silence that echoed beyond the day's event. The nervous energy these works unloaded could embrace innocence but, above all, ensnare tensions. They cut new ground.

In *Holding the Rope,* (1986), a little girl in a white dress walks forward, assisting in the 'celebration'. Sloan depicts her inclusion as an initiation rite where the child unknowingly will tread a disputed and marshalled route, as signified by the black-clad police who occupy the right half of the picture space. She eventually will enter the 'field'. Another work entitled *Entering the Field,* (1986), indeed has the aura of a holy place. Religion and land always co-habit in Ireland. The sky is dominant (less than a spacial quarter for the land) and marks the ground below with its turbulence — like a sign from God. Trust in God, within loyalism, is seen to ensure freedom and righteousness.

In *The Birches,* (1988), the artist applied the same overlay technique to explore more openly the landscape of rural Ulster — landmined as it is with the relics of history, religion and conflict. An apparently beautiful and peaceful region of small farmhouses near Portadown, The Birches, like other areas of rural Ulster has deep traces laid down, that Victor Sloan brought to the surface. Spectral images are always refusing to be laid down in his work where his prospecting technique is always rinsing them up.

In *Seek Me,* (1988), the biblical text attached to a tree claims its territory and acts as a flashpoint for the field to embody the marcher (the Orangeman) — an act of miraculous transubstantiation and revelation as provided by way of the secrets of the darkroom. From the same series of work both *Dogs,* (1988), and *Check-Point,* extend beyond the local terrain of Portadown to carry a charge that is all too easily recognisable from periods of suppression in 20th century European history. They fall into line with other events in other places; other claims on territory. Along with Willie Doherty, Victor Sloan[13] has offered us a new way of seeing, by way of a persistent and ultimately penetrating manner of questioning.

Primitive soundings; emergings of one sort or another mark and measure the 'art as journey' work of Deirdre O'Connell. The artistic journey, as with other Irish artists oscillates between the past (ostensibly Rome/Ireland) and the future (or is it the present?) — a boat is beached or abandoned; an armoured vehicle probes, on the brink here and there.

Her exhibition of drawings and sculptures *Insula/Peninsula* (ACNI Gallery 1990) was produced during and since her sojourn in Italy (1987/1988), as a Rome scholar (British School), in the city of church and pagan power. Public architecture, in one way or another is about power; buildings are never neutral, disinterested structures. O'Connell's work, while it was always about formal aspects of architecture, structure and skeletal rhythms, was also about enclosures/confrontations; insider/outsider acceptance and identity.

Rome's ancient buildings resourced new architectural drawings by the artist that have an atavistic comfort in their appeal but are also about ambivalence. In the *Pantheon Series* a coffered ceiling can be lightly raised off the surface in graffito crayon scrapings or in *Roma* a dome becomes a full breast or a nuclear head.

Ireland (Insula) and Italy (Peninsula) are on exchange. Notions of identity, culture, power and change (or lack of change) seep from drawing to sculpture; one to the whole. Enclosures becalm boats. *Beached Boat III*, a large charcoal and pastel drawing has a boat fixed as a picture intrusion balancing on the brink of some drained dam — a dependent vessel out of water.

There is an exquisite series of small drawings in earth reds, muted pinks and greys. *Rotunda* is a line drawing of some centralised church becoming a bulbous fluted object while the *Architect's Cupboard* houses favourite forms. It is not the language of classical primary forms but manncrist aberrations beloved by the likes of Richard Deacon or Anish Kapoor. Other drawings dig for skeletal boat remains emerging through grey/black charcoal, like fishbones.

Plaster is O'Connell's material where surface markings come up through the making process as inherent characteristics like board-marked concrete. Large white fragile pillars continued from previous concerns with towers and barriers. And it is not just the formal that is interesting here but the pursuit of narrative signs and reverberations calling or whispering from pillar to post. In some of these *Boat Pillars* (plaster and linen rag) the boat gets impaled and inverted. The vessel here, unlike its use in the drawings, has become petrified not to be refloated.

The artist's interest in understanding a material like plaster has been extended by way of Roman architecture. The sealed power (encodings) of Roman building is in the crude concrete aggregate between the brick sandwich. Now exposed it takes the building back to material essence. O'Connell has produced a series of structures, hand built as if by some colony of insects, with spiritual intentions. *Edifice I*, a simple cottage like dwelling, contrasts with *Chiesa*, (150 cm high) whose conical form carries the spiritual effect yet somehow mocking an ecclesiastical hat.

All of these works are left white to assist form and texture (most of her work uses neutrals) but recently she has impregnated the plaster with colour like fresco painting as in *Arca Assura* where colour is laid into the wet material like a watermark.

Back home, after Rome, a new series of drawings have started to merge suggested by the form and contents of domestic and industrial skips. These containers have become sealed vehicles with extended weapon-like antennae; they replace the open boat to move onto precipices like moon probes. Unlike the "Roman" oeuvre, we are not allowed in as yet. In the catalogue interview the artist claims:

'...In the drawings the skip is a vessel to purify, distil or extract, or is a convertor like the alchemist's apparatus.' [14]

The drawings, as yet, do not seem equipped to carry such claims.

Unlike the new wave of British sculptors in the 1980's, who are mostly men, (Alison Wilding a notable exception) in Ireland it is women who have emerged. Assured and articulate, they have invested the art object with a new lush sensualism or fabricated rich ideas and references. Deirdre O'Connell, after her Roman season, has joined the group.

The female body with Louise Walsh becomes the chief vehicle for expression to explore issues of gender, identity and politics and their interrelationships. In early works such as *Harvest Queen*, (1986) Walsh conjured a forceful bestiality in her amalgams of female and animal forms, sometimes on all fours. Moving from Cork to Belfast in 1985 the young artist was thinking about issues relating to sexuality; abortion, or the restrictions on its availability in Southern Ireland; the way women were being represented in the media and yet not given any power.

That's when the "beast of burden" notion came. I was trying to use a symbol that dealt with all my frustrations around women's bodies and feminism and I was really angry — all the work was due to anger.' [15]

The horse became her symbol of domesticated power; its wildness restricted, used and abused. Amalgamated with an open female structure, this hybrid form exuded great strength and resilience and a latent sense of rebellion. Walsh combined natural materials such as mud, straw, driftwood, bogwood with found objects. In *Harvest Queen*, (1986) a chain became the backbone, part of a rubber skeleton provided the anonymous face, while a laundry basket formed the rib cage. The creature, on her marks, was coiled and set for a mighty leap forward.

Her creatures would on occasions be raised upright like maenaids with the traces of embalmed entanglements running through them like shot circuitry. *Avenging Epona*, (1987) completed the series based on the deployment of the horse as symbol but the flying horse-goddess was, by now, no longer a victim but more a swooping dragon. Walsh often isolates the figure only to examine its silent and not so silent partners, abusers and controllers. Jenny Houghton has recognised the fragility of dependencies at work.

'Within Walsh's work is a sense of urgency, or energy and also an acknowledgement of the confines of self. Her work snaps open a welcome embrace of the frailty of the human condition and the reliance on others.' [16]

To that extent the artist can at times both mock and empathise with the generation gap — mother and daughter gender bindings. Her drawings are all linear entangle- ments of ideas and forms. Greek mythology is tapped for heroic birth scenes like Athena from the head of Zeus. States of being and power struggles emerge. If the sculptures are demonstrative in their bestiality and physicality, the drawings chart a more personal struggle. The mother/daughter relationship is here a grappling of expectations and rejections. In *Untitled Struggle,* (1989) the see-saw of the couples' arms simultaneously push and pull; they form a cradle-like boat. Indeed, in an earlier more comforting version on the same theme *And the Boat We Make Shall Keep Us Safe,* (1987) the younger earnest female leads and reluctantly the older figure is dragged along this eternal choppy sea voyage. Walsh views these drawings as a litany — a prayer for drawings.

Out Laws, In Laws, (1991), a work produced for the *In A State* exhibition at Kilmainham Gaol, dealt with homosexuality. The artist had been asked to respond to the idea of the state/the nation in the year that Dublin was acting as 'City of European Culture'. Walsh felt that it was totally hypocritical that the law in Ireland should still be intolerant of homosexual relations. The gaol is a symbol of English Imperialism in that it was the institution for incarcerating the Irish insurrectionists. Over the door are images of snakes restrained by the chains of Law and Justice. The snakes struck Walsh as very Celtic in their intertwinings and the operative notion of law very English. The snakes were deployed then, by the artist, as appropriate symbolism for a struggling sexuality as they once symbolised, in an Irish context, pagan threat.

The installation used a darkened cell in which the artist projected images of couples of the same gender kissing, with superimposed images of snakes curling, tattoo-like, across the faces. The images were disturbing and confrontational — their unease predicted as one walked over, or avoided, a glass covered hatch on the floor containing plaster snakes, before entering the cell.

'Although my snakes are under the surface I want them to be visible, numerous, struggling and unchained.' [17]

Walsh has continued to use 'constructed' photography in an environmental way in a collaborative work with Pauline Cummins called *Sounding the Depths,* (1992). By way of body language an ambitious progression of images eventually leads to a release — a speaking out. From a tight-lipped restraint we are led to a joyous celebration of feminist politics. The final sequence of images in cibachrome, showing reconstituted open mouth/torsos, hybrids, reminiscent of Sheelagh-na-gig self belief. Moira Roth in her catalogue commentary set the work within a strand of contemporary feminist art practice where the body, once subject of gaze, gazes back with a defiant confidence.

'I sense still somewhat inchoate, a renewal — perhaps more exactly phrased, a re-surfacing of the presence of the female body, frequently their own nude bodies, in art by a small group of contemporary feminist artists in different countries, different cultures. These artists have certainly done their theoretical readings on the problematics of such representations, yet each has — often for differing reasons — decided to return to her "country of the body", as Cummins so aptly described it.' [18]

Like Louise Walsh, Alice Maher unloads memory banks of an Irish female childhood. When Alice Maher moved to Belfast from Cork to study in 1985, a significant change took place. Drawing became central to her practice. In her M.A. degree show in Belfast she exhibited, separately, large drawings that were no longer preparatory or supplementary to painting but self-sufficient. From then on paintings, drawings and later installation work would cross-fertilise ideas; share investigations.

There is something of an exotic but somnambulistic journey going on in Alice Maher's work. In a series of mixed media works on paper the artist deals with child/woman change and interchange. These contrast with her more aggressive and overtly psycho-erotic drawings. There is a joy of colour making and trading in a Chagall-like surrealism and playfulness. *Hunting Them Home,* (1989) points to an absurd contrast between a child's acquisition of knowledge of the earthly animal farmyard and lack of reference to sexual relationships in the home. In *The*

Somnambulist, (1989) a wandering bride confronts the viewer from a garden of delights.

These fragmented, anti-logical narratives find three dimensional expression in a series of tents (*Tryst* series, 1989). In turn they are the sleepers, the dancers, the lovers and the procreation-places of refuge; private sound capsules. They arise from the mother provider/seamstress domain — textile as a tool of female stereotyping. But here the artist takes pleasure in the making and sewing. Colour stainings extend the female body analogy as points of departure for the creation and development of images on the move : a nomadic carnival. In earlier drawings there is usually a meeting of two or more forces, often in a disturbed state. In the series of drawings *The Thicket,* (1990), singular young girls do singular things before they become genderfied and get conscripted into roles. Maher, in these drawings, is reclaiming, repossessing this freer territory. In one drawing in the series, a girl, her hair falling around her, stares down a cone, a platonic form that could be dangerous. In another drawing the girl's hair forms a cylinder to envelope and concentrate a narcissistic reach towards her reflection from a pool — a private movement of vertigo. It is an awakening of the senses, as Penelope Curtis recognised:

'The Thicket series suggests, and derives from the senses. We experience the tentative touching, the lengthy looking, the inquisitive listening, the bolder exploration, the forthright destruction. The senses mean discovery, and in The Thicket Maher is concerned to validate our adolescent courage, and to give girls' adolescence the acknowledged status of the boys coming-of-age ritual.' [19]

Hair would continue to fascinate the artist, but in an even more theatrical way. States of change interest and compel Alice Maher: child/woman; growth/decay; interior/exterior. In her recent installation *Keep,* (1992), one central exploration, among the many allusions the work sets up, is that attitudes can change — systems of authority can change.

Keep is made from human hair gathered from hairdressers shops in Cork and Belfast, with donations from friends and contributions from the artist herself. It takes the form of a tower or pillar conditioned physically by the small top-lit space it occupied at the Old Museum Arts Centre, Belfast. Hair of many colours is interwoven into hanging braids or long ropes that define this cylindrical tower with its conical top.

The title of this interactive work *Keep*, reminds us of the Victorian practice of cutting locks of hair as keepsakes or mementoes. It also recalls the incarceration of the Brothers Grimms's Rapunzel and the networking of Maher's previous installation *Cell*, (1991) for the *In A State* exhibition at Kilmainham Gaol. But whereas *Cell* was about individual suffering and natural and spiritual decay, *Keep* seems more a joyous and hopeful invitation to explorations. In *Cell*, the spherical entanglement of brambles pushed out against the prison walls offering no invitation to enter this solitary confinement whereas one's extended arms can divide the hanging braids of hair and allow entry for more than one person.

Secret and secluded conversation have been offered by the artist in the colourful tents of the *Tryst* series. The textile material of these tents acted as vehicles for carrying imagery. With both *Cell* and *Keep*, Maher discarded the pictorial, if anti-logical, narratives of the tents for the illusory world of the invested object and its environmental interactions.

Each of us can make our own list of what *Keep* enmeshes and alludes to. But these would surely include the castration myths (e.g. Samson and Delilah); Medusa and the fateful gaze; St. Veronica; Auschwitz and, closer to home, the shaving of heads in the practice of tarring and feathering. And, if it can be read as 'a conversation piece' or Tower of Babel (heads being brought together), then it offers something to the resistance to political discourse in Northern Ireland. Once you enter and realise you can as easily exit, then you reject the work or process as a snare. The physical presence and symbolic nature of barriers, towers and defensive architecture have been explored in Northern Ireland by Irish artists and some from abroad; but Maher's tower is not about confinement but openness and enchantment.

The present generation of Irish artists are not content to celebrate either the landscape or the 'country of the body' and regard them not as given but constructed. Their approach is no longer, as in the past, a topographical journey but a subterranean quest. Hence the need for an art practice that was an open-ended but interrogating dialogue. The craft pleasures of picture making gave way to a series of land/body mining strategies.

FOOTNOTES

1. Brian O'Doherty, *Jack B. Yeats : Promise and Regret*, in *Jack B, Yeats, a Centenary Gathering* ed. Roger McHugh, The Dolmen Press, 1971, p.78.

2. Seamus Heaney, *Feeling into Words* in *Preoccupations*, Selected Prose, 1968-1978, Faber and Faber Ltd., London, 1980, p.52. See also Seamus Deane, 'Interview with Seamus Heaney (discussion on the role of the poet in politics)' in The Crane Bag, Vol. 1 No. 1, Spring 1977, ed. M.P. Hederman and Richard Kearney.

3. Aidan Dunne, catalogue essay Diarmuid Delargy, Prints and New Paintings, Orchard Gallery, Derry, 1989, p.9.

4. Ibid. p.17.

5. Interview with Marie Barrett, June 1992.

6. See Seamus Heaney, *Wintering Out*, Faber and Faber, London, Boston. See also P.V. Glob, *The Bog People*, London, Faber and Faber 1969.

7. Artists statement in Catherine Harper, A Beginning, exhibition catalogue, Orchard Gallery, Derry, 1991, p.7.

8. *Wintering Out*, op.cit.

9. D. Seymour, interview with the author 1993.

10. M. Farrell, as quoted by Cyril Barrett, Michael Farrell, Douglas Hyde Gallery, 1979 and Irish Times Interview, 1977, p.14.

11. M. Farrell, op. cit. p.15.

12. Brian McAvera, Victor Sloan's *The Walk, the Platform* and the *Field* exh. review, The British

Journal of Photography, 23rd May, 1986. p.624. See also *Direction Out* catalogue, Douglas Hyde Gallery, Dublin 1987, (unpaginated).

13. For discussion of other artists working with photography as a medium see B. McAvera, Magnetic North exhibition catalogue, Orchard Gallery, Derry, 1987.

14. Joan Fowler, (Interview with the Artist in Deirdre O'Connell Insula Peninsula, A.C.N.I., (exhibition catalogue), 1990, (unpaginated).

15. Conversation with the artist, May 1992.

16. Jenny Houghton, Louise Walsh exhibition catalogue essay, A.C.N.I. 1990, (unpaginated).

17. Artist's statement *Thoughts of Justice and Snakes*, In a State exhibition catalogue Project Press, 1991, p.59.

18. Moira Roth, *Two Women: The Collaboration of Pauline Cummins and Louise Walsh or international conversations among women*, Sounding the Depths, A collaborative installation by Pauline Cummins and Louise Walsh, Irish Museum of Modern Art, 1992, p.16.

19. Penelope Curtis, Strongholds, *New Art from Ireland*, exhibition catalogue, Tate Gallery, Liverpool, 1991, p.9.

Thou Shalt Not Kill

John Banville

Works of art have humble beginnings. They grow, like everything else, from a seed. Sitting at my desk recently, unable to work, I found myself thumbing through an old notebook, the one that I kept during the writing of my novel *The Book of Evidence*. The first page is dated 7 April, 1986. Here are the first new notes:

Notice in a cemetery (true): 'Planting and cultivation restricted to dwarfs.'

Browning's 'tender murderer'?

'There are no moral phenomena at all, only a moral interpretation of phenomena' — Nietzsche, *Beyond Good and Evil*.

(A small ad, clipped from a newspaper and pasted to the page:) 'Premature Baby Incubator, Vickers 59 for sale, as new. Offers, Box 402, Baby.

'The living being is only a species of the dead, and a very rare species' — Nietzsche, *Froliche Wissenschaft*.

Is it wrong to kill people? (underlined twice)

I do not think those cemetery dwarfs featured in the book, nor did the baby in its 'as new' incubator make an appearance, though they probably did lend the tale their own particular, subliminal touches of the macabre. Nietzsche is there in the pages, certainly, sometimes quoted directly, without acknowledgement — but not the two aphorisms that I have quoted from my notebook. Of course, the real origin of the book, the real gleam in the progenitor's eye, was that simple-seeming question: *Is it wrong to kill people?*

I am not a philosopher, not a psychologist, not a theologian, not a jurist. I address the subject of murder — or at least, the Mosaic injunction against murder — because I have written a series of three novels which together form an artistic meditation on the subject of a killing and its aftermath. The three volumes are *The Book of Evidence, Ghosts* and *Athena*. I did not set out to write a trilogy. Nor did I set out to write 'about' a murder (the work of art is never about something, though it may be about everything). I did, I suppose, have identifiable themes and ideas, which however loose and vague as artistic themes and ideas always are, could perhaps be grouped under the general heading, *The Search for Authenticity*.

The question of the authentic, of how to work authentically in a medium — art, that is — which at a certain level is necessarily fake, is one that obsesses the artist, consciously or otherwise. You take a square of stretched canvas and with infinite pains and manic concentration apply to it a series of multi-coloured daubs to make a pattern according to rigid but unknown laws: you arrange a series of sounds for voices or instruments or both combined, sounds which you may never hear outside your head (Schubert did not hear the bulk of his work performed), but which yet make a medleyed web in which an ineffable something is caught: you assemble a group of characters you have never known and will never encounter and make them dance their slow, intricate way through a story which is nothing like life — no novel is ever anything like life, though it may, as Henry James has it, *make* life — but which yet engages the reader as do those troubling dreams that come to us once in a while like succubi, drawing us into and out of ourselves, troubling our days — years, even — with the sensation of a reality more real than that which we experience in lived life itself. Where, is authentic; the territorial song of the oriole is authentic. But what of the sky painted from pigments? What of the imagined stone over which an imagined character trips as he hurries down the road to meet the love of his life? What of the stylised re-presentation of the bird's song in a piano piece by Messiaen?

You may think these matters only of significance, or interest, to the painter, the composer, the novelist, but you only have to ponder for a moment to realise that the problem of authenticity is at the very centre of the human predicament, and perhaps never more centrally located than in our, now closing, century.

So I set out, in *The Book of Evidence,* to invent an emblematic figure who in his actions and meditations would swing between the poles of the authentic and the inauthentic. I did not attempt to create what book reviewers would call an 'original' character — there are, as we all know, no original characters. This one had a particularly luxuriant family tree, with many an odd bird squawking among its branches. Dostoevsky's Underground Man is perched there, of course, sometimes in his own words (he figures darkly in that notebook of mine; 'Can a thinking man have any self-respect whatever?' he asks, and what thinking man can give an unequivocal answer?). The narrator of Sartre's *La Nausée* flexes a blue-black wing, and Camus's Meursault is heard every so often to sound a weary note. Nabokov's Humbert Humbert flashes like a firebird. Oh, there is a whole aviary here: Goethe's Werther. Buchner's Wozzeck. Kleist's Judge Adam. Wilde's Dorian Gray. Musil's brutish killer Moosbrugger ('if society could dream collectively,' says Musil, 'it would dream Moosbrugger'), and many, many more. Out of such bits and borrowings are characters made.

I gave him a name, at once ponderous and preposterous; Frederick Charles St John Vanderveld Montgomery. Usually a novelist — my kind of novelist, that is — will

I gave him a name, at once ponderous and preposterous; Frederick Charles St John Vanderveld Montgomery. Usually a novelist — my kind of novelist, that is — will infuse a character's name with as much resonance as it will bear: Godkin. Lawless. Grainger. Gabriel Swan, are some that I have employed. In this case I needed a name that would fall on the page with false resonance, or no resonance at all: Frederick Montgomery, *l'homme armée*, scion of a 'good' family, waywardly brilliant, self-regarding, dandyish, deceitful, feckless, vicious, murderous.

Freddie claims to have been in the far past, some kind of scientist, a mathematician, apparently. I am not sure that I believe him about this (I am not sure that I believe him about anything). In California, ten years before the time of the main events of the book, something occurs — or perhaps nothing occurs — and his life goes into crisis. Under this nameless affliction he is like Philip, Lord Chandos, in Hugo von Hofmannsthal's *The Chandos Letter*, who writes to his friend Francis Bacon: 'My case, in short, is this: that I have utterly lost the ability to think or speak coherently about anything at all.' My Freddie Montgomery can think, yes, and he can speak — by golly, how he can speak — but what is gone is coherence. Meaning has fallen out of his life like the bottom falling out of a bucket. Here he is, addressing the trial judge in particular and the rest of us in general, describing a pause on his way home from the Spanish island where he has been aimlessly footling away his life for years: the paragraph occurs early on in the book, but constitutes, nevertheless, a central moment:

A washed-blue dawn was breaking in Madrid. I stopped outside the station and watched a flock of birds wheeling and tumbling at an immense height, and, the strangest thing, a gust of euphoria, or something like euphoria, swept through me, making me tremble and bringing tears to my eyes. It was from lack of sleep, I suppose and the effect of the high, thin air. Why, I wonder, do I remember so clearly standing there, the colour of the sky, those birds that shiver of fevered optimism? I was at a turning point, you will tell me, just there the future forked for me and I took the wrong path without noticing — that's what you'll tell me, isn't it. you, who must have meaning in everything, who lust after meaning, your palms sticky and your faces on fire! But calm, Frederick, calm. Forgive me this outburst, your honour. It is just that I do not believe such moments mean anything — or any other moments, for that matter. They have significance, apparently. They may even have value of some sort. But they do not mean anything.

There now, I have declared my faith.

Freddie is obsessed with how thick is the texture of things that yet seem lacking in all substance. The world is solid as stone yet constantly quaking and shifting and sinking under him. He regards this world with the anguished fearfulness of a lover constantly in danger of losing the beloved. In this passage he is returning by ship to Ireland:

It was evening. The sea was calm, an oiled, taut meniscus, mauve tinted and curiously high and curved. From the forward lounge where I sat the prow seemed to rise and rise, as if the whole ship were straining to take to the air. The sky before us was a smear of crimson on the palest of pale blue and silvery green. I held my face up to the calm sea-light, entranced, expectant, grinning like a loon. I confess I was not entirely sober. I had already broken into my allowance of duty-free booze, and the skin at my temples and around my eyes was tightening alarmingly. It was not just the drink though, that was making me happy, but the tenderness of things, the simple goodness of the world. This sunset, for instance, how lavishly it was laid on, the clouds, the light on the sea, that heartbreaking, blue-green distance, laid on, all of it, as if to console some lost, suffering wayfarer. I have never really got used to being on this earth. Sometimes I think our presence here is due to a cosmic blunder, that we were meant for another planet altogether, with other arrangements, and other laws, and other, grimmer skies. I try to imagine it, our true place, off on the far side of the galaxy, whirling and whirling. And the ones who were meant for here, are they out there, baffled and homesick, like us? No, they would have become extinct long ago. How could they survive, these gentle earthlings, in a world that was made to contain us?

If Freddie Montgomery is obsessed by the world, half in love with its tenderness and beauty, and half in terror of its inexplicable insubstantiality, he hardly notices the people surrounding him. He compares them to mirrors into which he peers anxiously, searching for his own, hardly existent reflection (Count Dracula is another of his forebears). He comes upon a painting, and, in a passage to which he brings all his linguistic and imaginative skills, conjures a life for the long-dead woman who is its subject. Yet when, in the process of stealing the painting, he is confronted by a real, living woman, he bashes her head in, swats her out of his way as if she were no more substantial than a cobweb. *The Book of Evidence* is just what the title says it is; a presentation of the facts, not in any effort by Freddie Montgomery to prove his innocence or to excuse his murderous deeds, but as a kind of appalled act of witness. Look, he says to us, look, here is what happened! I can no more make sense of it than you can. When at the end of the book; after his capture, the police ask him why he killed the woman, he can only reply: 'I killed her because I could, what more can I say?'

As Freddie comes to realise, his *crime* was murder, but his *sin* was a radical failure of the imagination. We make others real only by imagining them: both the lover and the murderer know this. Yet where the lover and the murderer are different is that what the lover conjures into existence out of the white-hot furnace of his imaginings is a stylised image, a kind of magically detailed hologram of the beloved, while on the contrary, the murderer *makes the other real.* Here is Freddie dealing the first blow:

I turned to her. I had the hammer in my hand. I looked at it, startled. The silence rose around us like water. Don't, she said. She was crouched ...with her arms bent and her back pressed into the corner. I could not speak. I was filled with a kind of wonder, I had never felt another's presence so immediately and with such raw force. I saw her now, really saw her for the first time, her mousey hair and bad skin, that bruised look around her eyes. She was quite ordinary, and yet, somehow, I don't know — somehow radiant.

This immediacy, this radiance, are what the subject of the murder and the subject of the painting have in common. Although none of the critics has remarked it, this seems to me the real scandal at the heart of *The Book of Evidence*. The living, though soon to be dead, woman is no more real to Freddie — and to us — than the painted woman: less so, in fact. The border between art and life has become blurred and not just for Freddie. We too are somehow implicated in this crime.

Freddie Montgomery, under other guises, and other names, mediates on this failure of imagination, through *Ghosts,* which is an account of his time in Purgatory; and *Athena,* his attempt to set a new life in place of the one that he took. For all the passionate *looking* that takes place in *Athena* ('looking' being for Freddie a far more important act than that other act with which it indecently rhymes), the failure remains as it must. The dead cannot be made to live again, and art cannot be put in the place of life. Even so, he is determined that something will be salvaged from the disaster he has wrought — and wrought is the most suitable word here. At the end of *Athena,* when he has been abandoned by his love, and after he has discovered that although he looked and looked and *looked* at her, he did not succeed in seeing her, he is granted a final, fleeting vision.

I saw her yesterday. I don't know how, but I did. It was the strangest thing. I have not got over it yet. I was in that pub on Gabriel Street that she liked so much ... I was in the back bar, nursing a drink and my sore heart, sitting at that big window...that looks down at the city along the broad sweep of Ormond street. the street was crowded, as it always is. the sun was shining in its half-hearted way —yes, spring has come, despite my best efforts. suddenly I saw her — or no, not suddenly, there was no suddenness or surprise in it. She was just there, in her black coat and her black stilettos, hurrying along the crowded pavement in that watery light at that unmistakable, stiff-kneed half-run, a hand to her breast and her head down. Where was she going, with such haste, so eagerly? The city lay all before her, awash with April and evening. I say her, but of course I know it was not her, not really. And yet it was. How can I express it? There is the she who is gone, who is in some southern somewhere, lost to me forever, and then there is this other, who steps out of my head and goes hurrying off along the sunlit pavements to do I don't know what. To live. If I can call it living: and I shall.

✦ ✦ ✦ ✦ ✦

The most terrifying discovery in life is that we are free. Constrained, yes, but free. I sometime feel, in my darker moments, that the only truly interesting achievement of the human species — the most dangerous, the most terrible. species the world has ever known — is not the development of philosophy or religion, the application of science, the invention of romantic love, but the success with which we have ameliorated the horror we experience in face of our state of freedom. What stratagems we have devised to blind ourselves to the abyss that gapes always at our feet. What somersaults of logic we have performed, even on the lip of the precipice.

How are we to cope with that profoundly horrifying dictum of Nietzsche's I quoted at the outset, to the effect that 'there are no moral phenomena at all, only a moral interpretation of phenomena'? In the absence of a moral imperative, is it wrong to kill people? Religion is not much help, being itself steeped in the blood of saviours and martyrs and Philistines. Nor will art come to the rescue, as Freddie Montgomery can attest. Where, in Emerson's famous and characteristically ambiguous formulation. Where do we find ourselves? As I have said, I am not a philosopher, theologian, jurist. I have no pronouncements on the problem of evil, of the just war, abortion, euthanasia, capital punishment. All that an artist can do is present the evidence. *Here is what happened, this is how it felt, this is how the light fell, how the characters spoke: it is all made up, yet strangely real.* When I think of Freddie Montgomery and his dogged search for authenticity through the three novels that are, we may say, his creation. I return again and again to a brief little passage that occurs at the end of *Ghosts:*

> *I think of a picture at the end of a long gallery, [he says], a sudden presence come upon unexpectedly, at first sight a soft confusion of greens and gilts in the calm, speechless air. Look at this foliage, these clouds, the texture of this gown. A stricken figure stares out at something that is being lost. There is an impression of music, tiny, exact and gay. This is the end of a world. Birds unseen are fluting in the trees, the sun shines somewhere, the distances of the sea are vague and palely blue, the galliot awaits. The figures move, if they move, as in a moving scene, one that they define, by being there, its arbiters. without them only the wilderness, green riot, tumult of wind and the crazy sun. They formulate the tale and people it and give it substance. they are the human moment.*

It is one of the chief ironies of the trilogy that it is in those passages when Freddie contemplates the literally inhuman — the figures in paintings, or the figments of his own imagination — that he most closely approaches that state of full feeling humanness which is his one, consistent aim. Being a murderer, he must now, as he says at the end of *The Book of Evidence,* live for two. I am, he declares, 'big with possibilities'. He is pregnant with his own incipient humanity. He has learned to use his imagination, and, as Wallace Stevens has it 'God and the imagination are one'. It is not the God of Moses, that merciless slaughterer, but the god in our own heads that injuncts us: it is the imagination that commands. Thou shalt not kill.

Irish Music

Fintan Vallely

No doubt there are many mainland Europeans who are only vaguely aware of Ireland. Of them, most will not have consciously listened to Irish music. Those who have done so will certainly have heard of The Chieftains, and among them some will have been familiar with the 1960s ballad groups The Clancys, and The Dubliners, the 1970s groups Planxty and The Bothy Band. Others will know about De Danann, Stockton's Wing, Altan, Dervish, Nomos and the like. These will be aware too of soloists like Sean Maguire, Joe Burke, Sharon Shannon, Frankie Gavin, Maíre Ní Chathasaigh, and inspirational 'movers' like Donal Lunny and Arty McGlynn. Yet all these are only a tiny fraction of the playing musicians in Ireland.

Irish traditional music is a great swelling movement incorporating 'stay-at-homes' and compulsive wanderers, rigid conservatives and thrilling innovators, a syrupy, 'parlour' fussiness and a gritty, frontier edge. It has all the variety, conflict and contradiction of our political life, all the fanaticism, application and waywardness of a religion. As we now know it, it has taken shape within the last thirty years, parallel with and being nourished by major political upheaval in Ireland and Europe. And it has drawn on and contributed to the 'folk' revival movements of the western world. Through the efforts of hard-working individuals and lobbies it has patiently chiselled out a respected, substantial niche in our cultural self-image which is steadily developing its recognition by the state. Yet there is no one opinion common to all of its exponents, no clear picture of what the music is all about, or what what motivates them. Some have the resources within them to create new melodies, others are constantly on the prowl for ideas from elsewhere. There are those who consider that we are now on the cusp of perfection, those who are hung up on the supremacy of the recent revival-period, and yet more who consider the Golden Age to have died out within the last quarter of this century.

In the past, original creativity within this music has typically been concealed modestly by the tune and song makers, or at least passed off as unimportant. This is not only a consequence of the democratic, healthy begrudgery which keeps Irish people from getting big heads, but arises from the high level of interpretative creativity which is expected in even straightforward performance. Despite the absence of identified composers there are upwards of twenty thousand tunes and song lyrics in circulation, in print and on albums. In more recent years — a trend more noticeable in Irish America where there has been payment of royalties for public broadcast since the inception of radio there — pieces are being claimed by their makers. The small number of people so involved today suggests that there never were very many originators, more likely a sprinkling of highly-creative individuals with prolific output.

A tune is not like a piece of music in the classical tradition, however. As in popular music, the individual musicians playing it will each add their very particular stamp. Superior status is reserved for players, not for composers, and a good player is also one who can be identified by listening. Tunes, therefore, often gradually change over the decades as each successive interpretation adds or takes away some new element in the player's search for satisfaction. But if the piece is good enough, or at some point eventually becomes so, it will then remain in circulation unchanged. The process is not without control though. Particularly in the past, the community within which the player performed, for whom the playing was important entertainment, also acted as a litmus paper: if they liked it, it was requested again, if they didn't, it was ignored, fell out of use and disappeared.

These days though, the trend is for traditional musicians to claim their works in order to reap not only the financial benefits, but also to gain the accolades which the increasingly commercial world of traditional music is willing to give them. Prestige satisfies the ego, payment buys the freedom for the musician/singer to specialise. Such specialisation is now at an unprecedented level inside traditional music. Not only are there scores of professional musicians on circuits in Ireland, all over Britain and Europe, but also in the US and Canada, in Australia and New Zealand. Wherever Irish people have travelled, demand for traditional music is following; wherever in Europe the local culture is deficient in folk music, Irish music is attractive. The professionalism and specialisation produces more than performers. Among traditional music's wage-earners in this country have been the early radio personnel — collectors like the piper Seamus Ennis, presenters like National radio's Ciarán Mac Mathúna and more recently, television production staff like Tony Mac Mahon in Dublin, Tony McAuley in Belfast, presenters like Aíne Hensey in Clare. These people not only have been the useful, effective standards-setters, the arbiters of good taste, but because of the power of the role of one-station radio, they are now themselves music personalities. Arts Councils too in recent years in both Northern and Southern Ireland have had specialist traditional music officers to oversee the administration of grant aid and develop policy. Inevitably, the increasing commercial viability of the music has moved it onto a different economic plane which is represented most impressively by the 1994 Eurovision Song Contest *Riverdance* performance.

Riverdance began life as a short continuity spot of music by composer Bill Whelan, embellished by an Irish dance routine. It involved a large troupe of traditional dancers and 'star' traditional-based artistes Michael Flatley and Jean Butler. Truly electrifying and deeply moving, the public response to it took its instigators by surprise: a video of the piece sold astronomically, and *Riverdance, The Show,* followed, selling out a five-week, 1995 run of twenty seven performances at Dublin's huge Point Depot venue. That's an audience of 87,000, or one person in forty in the country. The number isn't unusual by comparison with football, or with London West End shows, but it is unique by indoor entertainment standards in Ireland: our biggest traditional-based singer, Christy Moore, did an impressive ten nights at the same venue in the same year, Mary Black and the Woman's Heart group did five, The Chieftains, on their own couldn't even think about it. Since then, *Riverdance* has been a hit in London and on Broadway. The thoroughly professional show has obviously brought a new paying audience on stream, much of which would appear not to have been active in traditional music in the past, who now not only enjoy it, but feel it as valuable to their self-esteem. It has liberated these people into a section of national culture from which they have in the past absented themselves, or have been excluded by deficiency in education policy, or just lack of confidence in the music. In so doing though, yet another dimension has been added to the complexity of the appeal of traditional music.

There is no doubt that commercial interests are prime movers in *Riverdance* — the Point Depot is a major music venue, and the advertising pitch by the promoters was colossal. But even believing that snowshoes can be sold to Australians, no mere PR pushiness could explain the evangelical sales-appeal of the big show, with its reputation based on a mere continuity slot in the mega-media, Eurovision song event. One can easily understand how Christy Moore could fill his 38,000 seats — he has been building a reputation and following for thirty-five years and has almost as many albums behind him. Allowing too for the successes of *Riverdance* composer Bill Whelan's earlier works, *The Seville Suite* and *East Wind*, it is still clear that something more fundamental must have been sparked by the particular combination of music and dance to be so corrallable by the advertisers, something that ran beyond mere familiarity with Irish dancing, perhaps something closer to the spirit of support for Ireland's soccer team over the last ten years.

This 'phenomenon' — judged to be so only by our past experiences within traditional music — reminds us that what is known as 'Irish traditional music' is now well and truly in the international recording limelight: uilleann piper Davy Spillane is promoted by Sony Music, the Donegal-based group Altan are now the protégés of Virgin/Atlantic. 'Big' money has moved into what was previously a scene of small independent labels, self-productions by artistes, and small gig fees dictated by the limited size of the music's one-time exclusively specialist audiences.

But the 'mass' market is an unfamiliar and contradictory place for a folk music to find itself, if only because 'traditional music' communities are normally either local, or united by a common aesthetic, a 'feel' for the interrelationships of players with their sources, audiences and their local history. All musics have their communities of course, but 'mass', or 'popular' are different — they occupy a territory defined by age group. Rock's is defined by age and era, jazz's (in Ireland) by dedication, class and self-image, Irish country and western's community is largely rural and defined by hands-on uncomplicatedness, art music's sphere is defined by class and education background. What, then, is different about 'traditional' music?

Let me illustrate by describing my own introduction to it. As a child I grew up in Catholic society in the countryside, close to the town of Armagh in present-day Northern Ireland. I say 'present-day', because my parents are of the pre-1921 All-Ireland, their political consciousness and cultural self-image — and hence that of their children — are rooted in that. 'Irish' identity in music for them, and for me growing up, was céilis and concerts, organised music performed by other people for dancing, or for listening. Around Christmas 1964, at the beginning of the popularity of ballads, at the age of fifteen, with absolutely no prompting, and not inspired by any mentor, peer-group, experience, family music background or backup, I bought a tin whistle and taught myself to play. By the following summer I was attending local music sessions, within a year I was taking part in Fleadhanna cheoil and had developed a circle of music acquaintances which was utterly invisible to my society in general. By the end of the decade I had won my laurels and was consciously part of a huge floating community of singers, musicians, dancers, conversationalists, drinkers, storytellers and real-life comics. If there wasn't a lift to the event in a car, then we travelled by bicycle: not even Miltown Malbay, Co. Clare, 300 kilometres distant, was too far. The music was compulsive, an addiction, we used talk about 'being bitten'. Our territory was the island of Ireland, our favoured spots were remote and romantic — Ardara, Swinford, Enniscorthy, Sligo, Thurles, Ballyvourney. These places gelled my rudimentary knowledge of Irish history, they were sites of living out Irish, national one-ness. Those place-names became the session, the 'night' or the Fleadh, and all became part of the substantial and perpetually-regenerating folklore and craic of the scene. This experience has also been that of many others in the years since.

This notion of community, of travelling, of a territory, is hugely important in traditional music: for its exponents and followers, it is their Ireland, a cultural sameness that transcends the mere border, surviving even in London and the Eastern USA. Irish Americans, English-Irish, Scots-Irish all feel it even more intensely. The music is a nation without frontier, but one which needs validation by the soil of an 'authentic' territorial base. After that, what is regarded as Irish music by those involved is better defined by what it is not. It is not pop, it is not rock, it is not country and western, it is not classical, it is not folk music of countries outside of Ireland, Scotland or England. A broad field, it is fundamentally acoustic, it is bounded on the one extreme by the banjo/mandolin/guitar-accompanied ballads found particularly in urban session venues, and especially strong and cohesive among émigrés On the other extreme is found the unaccompanied sean-nós singing in the Irish language. In between lies what is seen as 'traditional music' proper — unaccompanied singing in English (a repertoire largely borrowed from Scotland and England), and that great solid block of mostly dance melodies played on uillean pipes, flute, whistle, fiddle, harp, banjo, accordion, concertina, bodhrán harmonica and recently-introduced instruments such as guitar, bazouki and mandola. This music is performed socially and casually, semi-professionally and professionally, it involves a large spread of ability from poor musicians to a top elite of exceptional talent. Associated with it are the solo and choreographed 'step' dancing, and in particular 'set-dancing' — the Irish-ised quadrille and cotillion which date to the influence of 18th century France. Part of the music too, in varying degree, are of course singers like Paul Brady and Mary Black, and, still, the 18th century 'parlour' romantic national ballad style of Thomas Moore's melodies. In practice, each of these distinct interest-areas shades into to the next, with overlaps of taste and practice being common, but all are arranged, like the suburbs of a town girding a centre, around the tunes and songs that we have come to know as traditional music.

Whether they are involved in it or not, this block of traditional music — dance music, set dancing, unaccompanied song in English and Irish — is fairly clearly identifiable to most people in Ireland in much the same way as we can tell a Collie from a mongrel, a Nissan from a Ford. This despite the fact that all the techniques used in traditional song for instance — nasal embellishment, melisma, glottal stop, presence/absence of vibrato, tight throat/open throat, selective use of chest-cavity resonance — all are employed by rock, pop and western art musics and by other folk and classical, secular and religious musics. In instrumental music the same applies. What differentiates the 'traditional', musicians and singers will tell you, is, like Baloo the bear in Jungle Book, 'it's not what you do, but the way that you do it'. And the interpretations of that 'way' — the *nya* , as it is known — are what carve up traditional music itself into its different interpretative camps, adding to its dynamic by raising contradictions that produce different music expressions.

And so, *Riverdance* is seen by the hard-liners as only mimicking the 'real' music, using it as a cliché, a Match of the Day selection of dislocated and aesthetically-unconnected highlights. But what that big show more importantly brings to the fore is the new commercialism. Traditional music has always had a steady economic life. In late Medieval Ireland, harpers were professional, in the last two centuries uilleann pipers were on the professional stage and market sidewalk, for street singers and travelling musicians, music making was their source of income. This was a face-to-face exchange of music for money. Today, in stark contrast, the machinery of the entertainment world commoditises music — packages it and designs it for specific markets which are then convinced to purchase it. This is perceived by some of our thinkers as running against the sentiment of music's relevance to community. Even so, many traditional artistes like Altan and De Danann have quite some success commercially with straight, unadorned material, but few are in the 'big-time'. Within the music at this moment there are some five hundred different solo and group albums available (this a continuum from the beginning of recording in the nineteen twenties). In the past these have catered for a comparatively small market — anything from tens to tens of thousands. But recently the cross-genre — traditional style — *A Woman's Heart* album had sold over half a million copies up to the first half of 1995. In this camp, The Chieftains' albums are also high sellers — thirty-two albums still on the shelves, the last four wining Grammy awards. Most successful was their 1995 *Long Black Veil* which held eighteenth place for a fortnight in the US Billboard General Music charts and came into their World charts at number two, having sold more than two million copies. Successful too are albums by soloists Sharon Shannon and Liam O'Flynn. All of those, however, compromise by diluting their material with self-absorbed own compositions, including cajun, baroque, rock and other influences.

Commercial recording always commoditises the singer and the song, the musician and tune, performance frozen in acetate or plastic, potentially forever generating revenue. But the shelf-life does not only depend on the quality of the music, of the performer — it relies upon the PR machine promoting them. Traditional music generally sees 'the recording' differently: if it is straight-up music, backing and song, and it is successful — fine! There are few complaints. But, as with The Chieftains, if the traditional music becomes a background sound to set off other music, this is generally frowned upon. With *Riverdance*, Bill Whelan's tunes are considered nice, or even good by quite a few musicians, but nobody within the music believes that television and newspaper glitz about the show is anything other than hype, the observer and reader being conditioned what to think. This causes a degree of revulsion which is expressed as antagonism. To understand the minds of these critics — who are all vital parts of the music process which has created the big-time earners — it is necessary to look at what distinguishes traditional music from other popular musics.

Song, singer, performance and nostalgia all are important success ingredients in popular music. But while pop's nostalgia appears in its revived pieces, and is age-group related, in traditional it is era-generated and is intensely related to politics. Region, language, tradition and politics — supreme among them the political, to which the others all relate — are exclusive to traditional music and set it apart. Differing interpretations of these add further to the contradictions exposed by the current new wave of patronage of traditional music by commercial, market- driven aesthetics.

Regional style — the persistence of particular tune types, forms or stylistic devices in playing, choreography in dance, repertoire in songs and music — in most of Ireland has diminished in importance. Recording technology has brought all styles to at least the subconscious attention of all players, and has made these potentially available to them. Practically, most players now select the technique and repertoire they prefer. But in some areas — Donegal in particular — there is a conscious chauvinistic effort to preserve both the fiddle as supreme, and also the uniquely interesting style defined by the southern part of the region. Sliabh Luachra style, tied up with repertoire, types of tunes and a way of playing, has perhaps by now influenced the music of all of the considerable area of Cork and Kerry. That regional styles selectively and rejectively utilise and ignore particular playing techniques and devices is underlined by the uilleann pipes. In decline at the end of the last century, they were revived, and much was saved by the establishment of pipers' clubs in Dublin and Cork. Dying out again by the nineteen fifties, the work of Breandan Breathnach and the Na Píobairí Uilleann organisation brought them a new and popular status, but by then all players tended toward use of the collected pool of available technique. That is, piping itself became a community distributed over the whole island, individuals standing out on the strength of ability and charisma, rather than local accent. Today there are few local accents in music: the most noted are concertina style in Co. Clare, fiddles in Sliabh Luachra and South Donegal, flute in Sligo-Roscommon, song in Irish in Connemara, song in English in Ulster. There are however many, many individual and highly-personal styles of playing, which set apart the more unique players.

Language — the Irish language — is held in high esteem, or at least some degree of myth, by most traditional musicians. Even though most Irish people would like to be able to speak Irish fluently, this has as much to do with sense of identity and political memory as with love of language. Singing in Irish always produces a reverent silence, concert presenters and media personnel regularly preface their introductions with the clichéd cúpla focail (couple of words). Perhaps this is because the language was the tongue of those people who produced the music before the brutal Anglicisation which was a consequence of the appalling destruction of the 19th century Famine.

Language so shades into 'tradition' in music — that repetitive, handed-on practice of the local tunes in local styles, on favoured local instruments, for the entertainment and ritual-marking of successive generations of one community. Despite the fact that these days, no local communities have traditional music as their sole music expression, many do accord it a high pedestal in their self-identity. Instead, of equal importance there is a music community distributed throughout Ireland and areas of Irish migration abroad, which for the musicians and music lovers fulfils the same vital human function as religion does in a local community.

Politics is a difficult area. The most rudimentary simplification locates traditional music as the music of the

Irish people regardless of religion. While many songs, tunes, tune-types and some repertoire, are shared with Scotland, and other songs with England, stylistically, Irish music is different and has a different sound, playing practice, acceptability, social investment and loading and is therefore quite unique. Our folk music has been incorporated into our idea of 'nation-ness' no more recently than other cultural artefacts have been so incorporated in other countries right around the globe. As with those other places, particularly in song, the music has been invested too with our political history — constant opposition to incorporation with Britain and the UK, the folk memory of the '46 Famine in which a million died humiliatingly of starvation and disease while food was exported, and after which two million people emigrated. The late nineteenth century development of Irish nationalism, language and sporting organisations, the War of Independence from 1919-21 and all its battle memories, all are more recent associations. Small wonder that since the withdrawal of the British from the Republic in 1922 and our secession from the British Commonwealth in 1949, that this music should be regarded, fondly, as a uniquely Irish artefact. Its laid-back practice, like the lauded 'warmth', 'friendliness' and 'fecklessness' of the Irish people, is identified as the consequence of Catholic political culture (as in the notion of Catholic taste) as opposed to the stiff, self-denying, rational Presbyterianism which would ideally characterise Northern life.

However superficially or subconsciously, this spirit imbues traditional music, like folk musics everywhere — in Brittany, in Galicia, Pays Basque, Bulgaria, Chile, etcetera, it defines the folk against the establishment. It is their voice from the silence of dark history too, for it has also the added ingredient of containing somewhere within it the legacy of our lost, pre-16th century art music. More visible though are modern-day politics: Comhaltas Ceóltoirí Éireann, strongly nationalistic, the biggest organisation within the music, was set up in 1951, only two years after the declaration of the Republic. 'The revival' of the music has exactly paralleled the progress of the Civil Rights struggle in Northern Ireland, right through the 'Troubles' to the present day.

Not all musicians have this consciousness or bear these burdens, indeed most are only hazily aware of their country's history. But these are the ingredients of the motivating spirit which revived, revitalised and re-enfranchised the music within the last thirty years, and they are deeply ingrained in the consciousness of most musicians aged over fifty. The gimp (manner) of those people's performances — the stoic or sad demeanour — product of a 'serious' attitude to the music — general absence of public self-indulgence in playing — is passed on and recycled as one of the legitimate ways to express oneself. The nature of the most popular experience of the music — the session — itself is an utterly egalitarian commonage, with no deference to social class, and only the most subtle praise or acknowledgement given to superior talents. The session takes place on the one level, without a stage; essentially people play to each other as well as for themselves and listening participants, a generous site of practical democracy.

It is this aspect of the music which some people fear might be most destructively challenged by the new commercialism and its creation of high-earning, unreachable 'stars'. Yet, in practice, with few exceptions our musicians so far continue to be mutually accessible both musically and socially: they have transcended the designs of the commercial world and have retained their grip on humanity. This warm Bohemianism is a significant marker of traditional musicians, something that is greatly appealing to people in more rigid, selfish societies.

Further underlining the political and a sense of the past, this 'sharing of resources' attitude to music is indeed itself a consequence of the Famine and emigration. The

Irishmen and women who emigrated to the US in the last century maintained a closed community in the new world, keeping in touch through social events that were often built around music. So too in the big nineteen fifties emigration, music was an important cohesive force in New York and Chicago , and continues to be so today. The US diaspora has inspired too a wealth of new tunes in the last fifty years — tunesmiths like Ed Reevy and Martin Wynne have been followed by younger imaginations such as the prolific Liz Carroll. The variety of cultures in the United States has left musicians there more open to other music influences, so producing a versatility which gives us truly adventurous interpreters of tunes. Players like fiddlers Eileen Ivers and Martin Hayes, flute player Seamus Egan, accordionist John Whelan — all these combine intelligent and skilful adventure with a solid understanding of traditional music gleaned from being immersed in it since childhood. The performances and recordings of these players is experienced sometimes as threatening to older, native musicians back in Ireland, but often it is inspiring to the younger. But such players will say that are not reflecting their experiences in the world in which they live any more than the previous generation reflected their's.

And so it can be said that traditional music exists at two levels. It thrives in its subterranean world of dark, smoky bar sessions and concert halls, incubators of style and taste, their camaraderie, ambience and feedback sometimes inspirational to dazzling zeniths of performance. Associated with this is the more open Fleadh Cheoil scene which involves vast throngs of music lovers, players and competitors. Outside of both of these the commercial world coaxes and lures players and singers into marketable consistency and variety of sound that can be sold to the widest audience.

The two scenes presently co-exist quite happily, many musicians belonging to both, drawing the human warmth and historical comfort from the Fleadhs and the sessions, honing their skills and keeping alive by recording and playing concert tours. And both have always been part of the music. But the introduction of 'mass' music style may begin to have a detrimental effect early in the new century. For those of us who began to play thirty years ago, we learned from people who themselves learned in the pre-technology, pre-electricity era, for whom stories and anecdotes were a valuable component of performance, and for whom the music was to be treated reverently, with a sense of mystery, and indeed history. Most of their, and our, playing was acoustic, un-mediated and un-enhanced by electronics, ears tuned to the most delicate sound, the deliberate and sometimes pragmatic variation. Using recordings and big-stage concerts as primary source, today's young players hear themselves compete with impossible balanced sound and studio perfection. There is a legitimate fear that this guides players in the direction of exclusive stage performance, thereby undermining the democratic sociability and accessibility of the session and the Fleadh. Hugely impressive events such as *Riverdance* will undoubtedly bring new blood into traditional music, but this may well be impressionistic, superficial. It may also discourage and intimidate other bands and groups, and will siphon off their potential revenue with record consumers shifting their budget to more swish productions.

For years traditional musicians have argued painstakingly and somewhat successfully for State recognition for traditional music as it had been preserved by practice up to this point in time, as aural history, something carrying the keening of death, the wail of emigration, the triumph of gunsmoke and the good cheer of secular celebration — a highly-coloured resource of infinite potential. They were not arguing for its incorporation into the multinational commercial world, no more than the revolutionaries of 1916 were fighting to develop a tourism industry. Like the tourism, the commercialism of the music is welcome, but unlike tourism, it is now happening without the backup of any definitive intellectual reference structures. We indeed have a wonderful National Traditional Music Archive, we have a Folklore Department in University College Dublin, we have an officer in the Arts Council responsible for traditional music, and our Foreign Affairs department subsidises performance abroad by musicians, singers and dancers. But our primary schools cover little of it, and that only at the teachers' discretion. Second-level schools have no coherent programme to teach it, we have no specific undergraduate third-level degree course in it, and have only recently established a post-grad facility, this commercially backed. Our musicians and organisers have generated the exciting profile traditional music today enjoys, but when the advertising industry wears out by trivialisation the 18th century Carolan tunes, the bodhrán beats and the wailing pipes evoking bleak landscapes, there is a danger that, in the absence of education policy and structures, the music will shrink to its former level of inconsequence, and all the glamour of its present heyday be lost, its die-hard practitioners reduced once more to caricatures in their own territory.

In the television series *Bringing it All Back Home* a few years ago, rock, popular. country and traditional music were juxtaposed, their best-known figures verbally complimenting each other for mutual inspiration. But the feeling among many traditional musicians, despite the media's favouring 'fusion' and integration of music genres, is that there is no comfortable overlap of the traditional and the popular — they are fundamentally different. What seems to unite them most at this moment is not compatibility, or even similarity, but only the commercial success of each's top-earning performers. Rock/pop have yet to demonstrate what they can usefully offer traditional; on the contrary, they have much to gain from, and are hugely attracted by the fresh, ethnic buzz of the traditional, as a new resource for what could be called 'anecdotal music' only — the tourist's wonder at the round tower while the local people stand invisible and ignored, so to speak.

Traditional music's role is changing. But that does not mean that its suffocation by pop/rock is inevitable. In its original dance function the purpose in playing was to provide a structured rhythm to be patterned in recreational dance-steps. Melody was built around that rhythm, or the required rhythms built into the melodies. The first priority was that the music be heard, and this was achieved by the players sitting on a table or some platform, or two or more musicians playing together to increase volume, thus prompting the formation of bands. Despite the survival of set and step dancing, and despite popular revivals, for some forty years now we have had such a huge variety of modern dances which are infinitely more appealing to the younger, transient, sub-cultures that the dance role for traditional music became largely redundant, contributing to the bulk of present-day Irish music being produced for listening. This is reflected in the number of albums available.

The other significant change in the music is that the revival coincided with the migration of the rural poor, the educated children of the agricultural petit bourgeoisie, to the cities and towns. Most of our non-professional musicians are now urban based, most have professions — teaching, media work, technical, administrative, etcetera — they are the urban middle classes. Their incorporation into the structures of State, into local government and central government positions of political, social and economic power, is possibly the biggest reason for traditional music's creeping official recognition. It is also probably the reason why there is an apparently new 'respectable' audience out there to patronise *Riverdance* and other high-price concerts.

But the changes in the fortune of traditional music are courtesy of other factors too, notably economic and political. First, increased prosperity in Ireland since the advent of the EC has produced the disposable income necessary to pursue such an expensive pastime as music. For it costs money to get instruments, send children to classes, for travel, food, accommodation and entertainment at sessions and fleadhs. Second, the idea of economic independence becomes increasingly irrelevant, submerged as we are in the European community. Standardisation of products and the availability of all branded goods everywhere make it all the more pressing to have clear, refreshingly different markers of national identity. We do not speak our own language as a nation, but what we do have is a music, hence its increasing importance to us.

Our musicians and cultural lobbyists are wary of submerging the traditional in what they see as the myth of Irish rock/pop, an evolved industrial genre of music which has little to do with Ireland as a country, and much to do with the forces which obliterate distinctiveness in other cultural areas. Some of the new developments in music are catchy and appealing, especially so, perhaps, to jaded, muzak-battered European eardrums. But we are concerned that we should not just be satisfying a 'lowest-common-denominator' demand from people who have lost their sense of finesse, who know no better, settling for an ephemeral, short-term, mass commercialisation and/or exploitation of the traditional arts, which with their passing away — like other music and dance fashions — will leave our world spent, colourless, and devalued.

Still, traditional music in Ireland benefits from jockeying for credibility with State and media, our performers taking a certain comfort from the control-free, artistic space so created. The music offers a huge variety of styles, instrumentation, energy and tempo. It provides entertainment which is not superior, is accessible, challenging to both listener and performer, demanding attention and interaction, is not obscured by mass-music, by karaoke delivery. Most importantly it offers this acoustically, with great mobility and versatility. The sites of its performance are uncluttered and unpressurised, not rendered remote and unreal by the Mardis Gras mask of electronic mediation. It is conducive to socialising and conversation. Its hundred and more weekend festival gatherings of song and music every year in Ireland provide our largely urban-based population with not only the potential to escape from the humdrum of city noise and streetscapes, but also exert a certain pressure to make us travel to another region. They challenge us to treat our ears to refreshing accents, relax our eyes on new landscape, to hear something new while exercising our arts constantly and in the company of different people.

BIOGRAPHICAL NOTES

EAVAN BOLAND is a poet, whose works include *The Journey*, *Selected Poems*, and *Outside History*.

JULIA O'FAOLAIN is a writer and novelist, born in Ireland and now living in London. Her books include *Women in the Wall*, *No Country for Young Men*, and *Melancholy Baby*.

BOB QUINN is a writer and filmmaker, whose works include *Atlantean* and *Smokey Hollow*.

ANGELA BOURKE is a writer and Lecturer in Modern Irish at University College, Dublin. She has published extensively in Irish and English on aspects of Irish tradition, and also writes fiction in both languages.. Her short story collection, *By Salt Water*, was published in 1996.

FINTAN O'TOOLE is a writer and columnist with the *Irish Times*. His books include *Black Hole, Green Card*, *A Mass for Jesse James*, *Meanwhile, Back at the Ranch*, and *The Ex-Isle of Erin*.

JOHN HUME is the leader of the SDLP and an MP and MEP.

LIAM KELLY is an art critic and Visual Arts Organiser of the Orchard Gallery in Derry. His books include *The City as Art*.

JOHN BANVILLE is a novelist and Literary Editor of the *Irish Times*. His most recent novel is *The Untouchable*.

FINTAN VALLELY is a traditional musician and freelance writer on Irish music. He lectures on Irish and international folk music at the NUI Maynooth.

PAUL BRENNAN is Professor of Irish Studies at the University of Caen, Director of Research at the Sorbonne Nouvelle, and president of the Société Francaise d'Études Irlandaises (SOFEIR). His books include *Civilisation Irlandaises* and *The Conflict in Northern Ireland*.

CATHERINE DE SAINT PHALLE is a novelist. Her books include *N'écartez pas la brume!* and *Moby*.